THE
RISE & FALL
OF
JIM CROW

THE
RISE & FALL
OF
JIM CROW

The African-American Struggle Against Discrimination, 1865–1954

By Richard Wormser

FRANKLIN WATTS
A Division of Grolier Publishing
New York London Hong Kong Sydney
Danbury, Connecticut

To Annie, for everything

IMPORTANT NOTE TO READERS: This book includes quoted material from speeches, letters, and other primary sources, that contains instances of derogatory terms and inflammatory language. In the interest of historical accuracy, these excerpts have not been altered; they reflect the usage of the period. The author and the publisher condemn the use of such language out of its historical context.

Visit Franklin Watts on the Internet at:
http://publishing.grolier.com

Library of Congress Cataloging-in-Publication Data

Wormser, Richard.
The rise and fall of Jim Crow: the African-American struggle against discrimination, 1865–1954 / by Richard Wormser.
p. cm
Includes bibliographical references and index.
Summary: Discusses the laws and practices that supported discrimination against African Americans from Reconstruction to the Supreme Court decision that found segregation to be illegal.
ISBN 0-531-11443-0
1. Afro-Americans—Segregation—History—19th century Juvenile literature. 2. Afro-Americans—Civil rights—History—19th century Juvenile literature. 3. Afro-Americans—Segregation—History—20th century Juvenile literature. 4. Afro-Americans—Civil rights—History—20th century Juvenile literature. 5. United States—Race relations Juvenile literature. [1. Afro-Americans—Segregation—History. 2. Afro-Americans—Civil rights—History. 3. United States—Race relations] I. Title.
E185.61.W935 1999
305.896073—dc21
99-28254
CIP

CONTENTS

1. THE JUBILANT DAYS OF FREEDOM   9

2. CONGRESS INTERVENES   18

3. FROM RESTORATION TO "REDEMPTION" 1870–1880   30

4. EDUCATION: A ROAD TO FREEDOM   41

5. JIM CROW COMES TO TOWN   48

6. DISFRANCHISEMENT   55

7. THE DARKEST TIME   67

8. UPLIFT   79

9. REBELLIONS, RIOTS, AND STRIKES 1900–1913   85

10. THE EMERGENCE OF W. E. B. DU BOIS   90

11. JIM CROW AMERICA 97

12. FIGHTING BACK: VICTORIES AND DEFEATS 105

13. THE WALLS COME TUMBLING DOWN 116

14. VICTORY 125

EPILOGUE 132

SOURCE NOTES 135

INDEX 140

THE
RISE & FALL
OF
JIM CROW

An 1865 engraving shows the history of blacks in America (counterclockwise from the upper left), from the arrival of the slave ships, to the promise of emancipation (center), above the guiding spirit of Abraham Lincoln.

ONE

THE JUBILANT DAYS OF FREEDOM

Jim Crow: 1) A stereotype Negro in a song-and-dance act presented by Thomas D. Rice [in the 19th century]. 2) discrimination (as in educational opportunities, social rights or transportation facilities) against a racial group other than white, and especially against the Negro in the Southland by either legal enforcement or traditional sanctions. . . .

———*Webster's Third International Dictionary*

APRIL 2, 1865. A group of enslaved men and women in Richmond, Virginia, huddle together, chained inside a jail. Tomorrow, they are to be sold down river to Mississippi. As daylight slowly pierces the barred windows, the prisoners wake to the sound of military drums. Peering outside, they see a remarkable sight—an army of liberation marching down the street! The United States 28th Colored Troops, led by Chaplain Garland White who had once been enslaved himself, has entered Richmond. The unit stops before the jail, and Chaplain White begins to address the gathering crowd.

> *I found myself called upon to make a speech. A vast multitude assembled on Broad Street, and I was aroused amid the shouts of ten thousand voices, and proclaimed for the first time in that city freedom to all mankind. . . .*

As he speaks, a song bursts forth from behind the prison walls.

Slavery chain done broke at last!
Broke at last! Broke at last!
Slavery chain done broke at last!
Gonna praise God till I die.

I did tell him how I suffer
In the dungeon and the chains
And the days I went with head bent down
An' my broke flesh and pain.

Garland describes his reaction:

I became so overcome with tears that I could not stand up under the pressure of
such fullness of joy in my own heart. I retired to gain strength.

In hundreds of towns and cities, and on plantations throughout the South, black men and women celebrate what some call the Day of Jubilee—the long-promised time when God liberates his people. One woman remembers:

I jump up and scream, Glory, Glory, hallelujah to Jesus. I'se free, I'se free.
Glory to God, you come down and free us. De soul buyers can nebber take my
two children from me, nebber can take 'em from me no more.

Almost four million African-American men and women once regarded as property are free. Technically, President Abraham Lincoln freed all those held in captivity in Southern states when he issued his Emancipation Proclamation on

African-American soldiers
liberate a Southern city.

January 1, 1863. But freedom becomes a reality only when the Union wins the war.

Even as the freedmen and women enjoy their freedom, they are confused and uncertain. Much remains to be resolved. Where will they work? How will Southern whites treat them? Where will they find homes? Will they be able to own land? Will their children receive an education? What political power will they have? To help them, Congress authorizes the Freedmen's Bureau in March 1865. Its full name is the Bureau of Freedmen, Refugees, and Abandoned Lands. Administered by the army, the bureau is to organize a system of free labor, settle disputes among blacks and between whites and blacks, administer confiscated land, ensure that blacks receive justice in the courts, and establish schools. It is aided by northern churches that send thousands of ministers—both black and white—and missionaries and teachers south with Bibles and spellers to help "uplift the race." Many of these men and women are abolitionists who have long opposed slavery.

African-American soldiers, many of them runaways from Southern plantations, fight for freedom during the Civil War.

William Channing Gannett, a white missionary from New England, observes that while blacks welcome white assistance, they do not want white control:

They have a natural praiseworthy pride in keeping their educational institutions in their own hands. There is a jealousy of the superintendence of the white man in this matter. What they desire is assistance without control.

Many newly freed men and women realize that the main responsibility for their future lies with themselves. Education is one of their first priorities. Booker T. Washington, who was born in slavery and whose climb up the educational ladder is to become legendary, voices his people's passion for education.

To get inside a schoolhouse would be about the same as getting into heaven. Few people who were not right in the midst of the scenes can form any exact idea of the intense desire which the people of my race showed for education. It was a whole race trying to go to school. Few were too young, and none too old, to make the attempt to learn.

African-Americans are eager to build their own churches too. Churches are the heart of the community—not only spiritual centers, but social, educational, and political centers as well. Many black congregations that, under slavery, had been subject to white ministers and churches immediately either withdraw from white churches or take control. In 1867, the black membership of the Methodist church in the South is 40,000. Six years later it drops to 653. In 1858, there are 25,000 black Presbyterians. By 1875, the number is 1,614.

Blacks set up benevolent societies to take care of the sick and elderly. They form social organizations, dramatic societies, debating clubs, fire companies, militia groups, and temperance clubs. They hold parades and celebrations and agitate for civil rights, political power, and justice in the courts. There is so much activity that one man comments, "We have progressed a century in a year."

From Emancipation through Reconstruction, African-American men, women, and children gather to voice their desires for land, civil rights, and a part in the political process. The meeting place is often the church, which is also used for dealings with the government.

Restoring broken families is another major priority. During slavery, tens of thousands of children and parents, brothers and sisters were cruelly separated. After the war, men and women walk hundreds of miles in search of lost relatives.

As African-Americans build institutions, they debate their future. Men,

women, and children draw up petitions expressing their hopes and desires. At the
1865 Convention of the Colored People of South Carolina, the delegates request

> *that we shall be recognized as men; that the same laws which govern white*
> *men shall govern black men; that we have the right of trial by jury by our peers;*
> *that no impediments be placed in our way of acquiring homesteads; that...we*
> *be dealt with as others are—in equity and in justice.*

Land and justice are the pillars of their newly found freedom. Without land,
many feel there can be neither justice nor freedom. Many argue that it is only right
they be given the land that they once worked without pay. Without land, they can
never be free. As one freedman explains to a Northern journalist:

> *Every colored man will be a slave and feel himself a slave until he can raise his*
> *own bale of cotton and put his own mark on it and say, this is mine. Without*
> *independence and self-employment, freedom would be meaningless.*

The Freedmen's Bureau distributes confiscated and abandoned plantations in
Mississippi and the Sea Islands to some 10,000 newly freed families. But President
Andrew Johnson returns all confiscated lands to their former owners two months
after the war ends. The very thing that blacks fear—domination by Southern
whites—begins to happen. One white planter predicts:

> *The nigger is going to be made a serf as sure as you live.*
> *It won't need any law for that. . . . They're attached to the soil and to their*
> *masters as much as ever. I'll stake my life, this is the way it will work.*

Sidney Anderson, a Northern journalist traveling through the South, finds most
whites obsessed with blacks: "Everybody talks about the Negro, all hours of the day

and under all circumstances. What would become of him? How would he survive? Where would he work? What could he do? And would he take revenge?" Southern whites complain about the way African-Americans exercise their freedom. They are enraged by the presence of black soldiers guarding their towns. They are annoyed by the independent attitudes of the men and women they once held in bondage. They are furious when blacks refuse to yield the sidewalk, or ride a mule or carriage in their presence. Whites accuse blacks of being "disrespectful," "insolent," "insubordinate," and "ungrateful."

White anger builds when blacks resist efforts to control their lives. Whenever they can, blacks insist that they work fewer hours than under slavery, that they be paid for nonfarming jobs and be given some land to work for themselves, and that schools be provided for their children. They want their wives and daughters to remain at home rather than work in the fields. At times, they walk off plantations and refuse to sign contracts for a new year. When some planters refuse to compromise, they find their barns or homes burnt down. On some plantations and in some cities, black workers go on strike. In New Orleans, black workers join forces with white workers to strike for higher wages.

Whites fear that blacks will no longer work for them. Cotton is still the main crop of the South, and white landowners have no other source of labor than black workers to plant, "chop," and pick cotton. "I never did a day's work in my life," one planter says, "and I don't know how to begin." White women are terrified of losing household servants. Many do not know how to cook dinner, clean house, or wash and iron clothes.

In almost every Southern state, white legislators begin to pass a series of laws known as the "black codes," restricting black workers and forcing them to work the whites' land. If a black man is found to be unemployed, he is arrested as a vagrant and fined. If he fails to pay that fine, he is turned over to a planter who pays it and then forces the man to work to pay off his fine. Blacks who break work contracts can be sold into labor for one year. Orphans and even children of families can be taken away from their homes and forced to work. To ensure that blacks remain farmers and servants, whites bar African-Americans from seeking anything other than agricultural or domestic work without special licenses. They cannot live in towns or cities without white permission. They cannot lease, rent, nor buy land. The codes also deny African-Americans the right to vote, hold office, and travel where they want. They must pay special taxes that cripple them and allow the state to send them into forced labor. Congress and the Freedmen's Bureau require white Southerners to withdraw the codes, but many planters continue to whip and beat their workers as in the days of slavery.

Attempts that blacks make to assert equality are often ruthlessly suppressed. For many whites, seeing their former slaves educated is worse than seeing them free. Southerners are afraid of what educated blacks might do. A Southern senator warns, "Keep the spelling book and the land from the possession of the Negro if you hope to control him." Southern planters know that an educated black man may refuse low manual labor and seek jobs that whites feel belong to them.

Some states pass laws dividing public spaces into white and black sections. Some streetcar conductors and steamboat conductors refuse to allow blacks to ride. Blacks are banned from most theaters and restaurants. They are denied justice in the local courts. A black man convicted of stealing a shirt worth $8 is sentenced to three months in jail, while a white man who steals a pair of shoes worth $13 is fined $2.

Racial tensions lead to whites murdering blacks in unprecedented numbers, often with great savagery. White men murder blacks for any reason or no reason at all. One man explains that the victim "didn't remove his hat." Another says he "wanted to thin out" the black population. A third remarks that he wanted to see the victim "kick." Bodies are mutilated, ears severed, tongues cut out, eyes gouged, and men beheaded and skinned, with the skin nailed to the barn. In Memphis, New Orleans, and Charleston, race riots explode as federal troops stand by and refuse to intervene. In the countryside, night riders whip and murder blacks and their white supporters. Black soldiers or former soldiers are often singled out. Whites cut their throats or shoot them in the head. Black landowners are another target. They are whipped, beaten, or driven out of their homes or off their lands. Whites who commit these murders, many of them known to all, go unpunished. Colonel Samuel Thomas, the Freedmen's Bureau Commissioner in Mississippi, observes that Southern whites have no regard for black rights:

> people . . . are unable to conceive the negro as possessing any rights at all. Men who are honorable in dealing with their white neighbors will cheat a negro without feeling a single twinge of their honor. To kill a negro they do not deem murder; to debauch a negro woman they do not consider fornication. . . . The whites esteem the blacks their property by natural right . . . and . . . they treat the colored people just as their profit, passion, or caprice may dictate.

The conflicts reveal to Sidney Andrews that Southern whites are determined to return African-Americans to slavery:

> If the nation allows the whites to work out the . . . Negro's future in their own way, the condition in three years will be as bad as it was before the war. The viciousness that could not overturn the nation is now mainly engaged in the effort to retain the substance of slavery. What are names if the thing itself remains?

TWO

CONGRESS INTERVENES

AFTER ABRAHAM LINCOLN is assassinated, Andrew Johnson promises blacks that he will be like Moses to them. In reality, he is closer to Judas. He turns his back on their desire to own land and to have rights and persons protected under law. Johnson wants the South reconstructed—that is, reorganized—and brought back into the Union under white control. Although he opposes slavery, he does not believe in racial equality. "I believe they [African-Americans] have less capacity for governing than any race of people on earth," he says. He eventually pardons most Confederate soldiers and officers, allowing many former Confederates to be restored to power as long as they take the oath of allegiance to the United States.

Since Johnson does nothing to interfere with white rule, the South tries to restore slavery in substance if not in form. At first, there are few objections from the North. Congress has granted blacks civil rights, but most Northern states refuse to allow them to vote. Most Republicans are willing to allow the South to deny blacks the right to vote, but will not tolerate injustice and violence. To many Republicans, the South is acting as if it had won the war and is defying the North—with Johnson's blessing. Some Southern states go as far as to elect prominent Confederate leaders to the Senate and Congress. The Republican-controlled Congress refuses to accept their credentials and denies them seats.

Republican leaders first try to get Johnson to compromise. If Johnson promises to protect blacks' civil rights, Congress will not push for voting rights. Johnson—stubborn, hostile, and believing he has the country behind him—refuses to compromise. A showdown is inevitable.

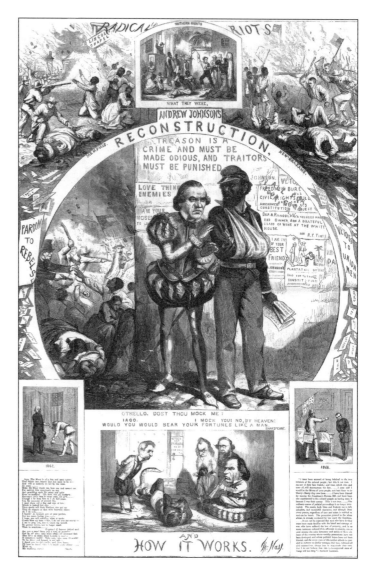

An 1866 engraving shows the betrayal of the promise of emancipation, with President Andrew Johnson portrayed as the false friend Iago, from Shakespeare's *Othello*.

The heart of the Republican-controlled Congress is a group of senators and congressmen known collectively as the Radicals. Many of them are from New England and were active in the abolition movement before the war. Others come from anti-

The Radical Republican Thaddeus Stevens (standing, at the right) was a member of a congressional Joint Committee of Fifteen that struggled with President Johnson for control of Reconstruction.

slavery sections of states such as Illinois, Pennsylvania, and Ohio. While the Radical Republicans are a minority in their own party, they have tremendous influence.

In 1866, Congress passes a series of laws eliminating federal and state discrimination. Congress also repeals a federal law that bars black people from carrying the mail. It allows African-Americans to testify in federal courts and sit in the visitors' galleries in Congress. The first black lawyer is accredited to the Supreme Court. Congress also passes two major bills that deeply affect the South. One is a civil rights law that states that all native-born Americans (except, ironically, for Native Americans) are entitled to certain basic rights, including the right to sue; to make contracts; to inherit, buy, purchase, and hold land; and to enjoy "full and equal benefit of all laws." To ensure that a future Congress will not undo the bill, the Republicans also pass the Fourteenth Amendment, which constitutionally guarantees citizenship and due process of law to all persons born in the United States. The amendment also disfranchises, or takes away voting rights, from those who served in the Confederacy during the war until such time as Congress restores their voting rights.

The Civil Rights bill is needed because of the growing violence against blacks in the South, yet President Johnson vetoes it. A showdown between Johnson and the Congress comes in the Congressional elections of 1866. The Republicans overwhelm the Democrats and Johnson, and end up controlling more than two-thirds of Congress. With enough votes to override any presidential veto, the Republicans pass the civil rights law.

Congress now takes over Reconstruction. Motivated by a sense of injustice as well as a desire to increase the Republican voting base, they move to make black men full citizens of the United States. They pass legislation giving African-Americans in the District of Columbia the right to vote. They then extend this right to blacks living in the Western territories. Congress also shocks the South by passing the Reconstruction Act, which divides the former Confederate States into five military districts. The general in charge of each district is to prepare the states in his jurisdiction for readmission to the Union by registering all citizens, black and white. They are then to order elections for conventions to adopt new state constitutions

The Reconstruction Act of 1867 divides the South into five military districts. (Tennessee rejoined the Union earlier.)

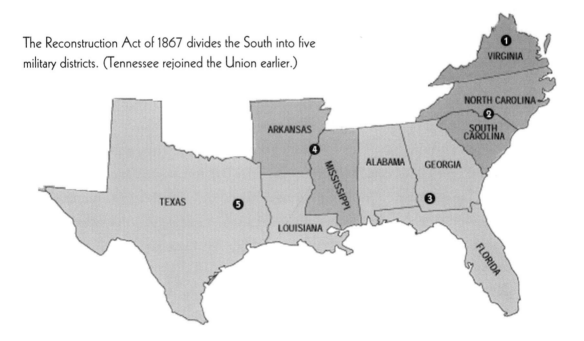

that must give black people the right to vote and protection of their civil rights. To be readmitted to the Union, every Southern state has to approve the new provisions and ratify the Fourteenth Amendment. In 1868, constitutional conventions are called in almost every Southern state. Black voters are fully represented for the first time and African-Americans campaign with great enthusiasm. They stage parades and celebrations, picnics and rallies.

The white South, however, is enraged at being forced to enfranchise blacks. Governor Perry of South Carolina writes Congress an angry letter:

> *The radical Republican Party forgets that this is a white man's government and created for white men only; and that the Supreme Court of the United States has decided that the Negro is not an American citizen under the Federal Constitution. Each and every state of the Union has the unquestionable right of deciding who shall exercise the right of suffrage.*

The Republicans make it clear that until the Southern states accept their conditions, they will remain under military rule. Congress hopes this will ensure that African-Americans can become full citizens of the United States, with all civil and political rights. Senator Richard Yates proclaims, "The ballot will finish the Negro question. . . . The ballot is the freedman's Moses."

On paper, the new state constitutions promise much. They guarantee blacks equal civil and political rights, and establish schools, prisons, and asylums for both races. They remove many of the restrictions against blacks and outlaw many of the harsh punishments such as whipping. African-Americans are guaranteed the right to sit on juries and testify in courts in most states. Poor whites as well as blacks benefit from the new constitution.

Most constitutions avoid the issue of equal treatment in public places and on transportation, as whites are bitterly opposed. Many blacks are willing to accept separation temporarily if they can control their own schools, churches, and social organizations. Their hope is that, in time, they can create a truly democratic, integrated multiracial society.

Even as blacks triumph, signs of trouble appear. One planter predicts what is to come:

> *Let not your pride nor yet your pretended friends flatter you in the belief that you ever can or ever will, for any length of time, govern the white man of the South. Your present power must surely and soon pass from you. Nothing that it builds will stand, and nothing will remain of it but the prejudices it may create.*

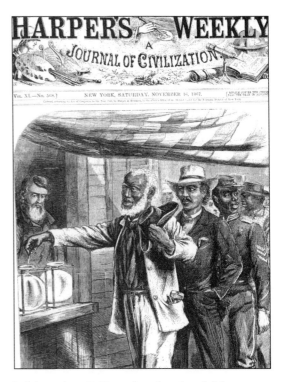

In November 1867 newly enfranchised African-Americans vote in large numbers.

As the Radical Republicans take charge of Reconstruction, a tremendous burst of political energy is released in the black community. In every city and town, politics becomes the main preoccupation of African-Americans. One planter observes, "You never saw a people more excited on the subject of politics than are the negroes of the South. They are perfectly wild." Black ministers feel that politics is replacing religion. "Politics got in our midst, and our revival or religious work for a while began to wane," one minister complains. To counter this, ministers begin to preach the Republican Party alongside the Bible.

But while African-Americans are now active in Southern politics, they are a minority in many states. Most Southern whites support the Democratic Party, the

Southerners see the invading Northerners as greedy carpetbaggers.

party of white supremacy. To gain political power, blacks have to join forces with those whites willing to support the Republican Party and black rights. Many of these whites are Northern Republicans who migrate to the South after the war—to perform religious educational work among the former slaves, or to make their fortunes, or both. Some are confidence men who will become notorious for their corruption. White Southerners contemptuously call them "carpetbaggers," a name borrowed from the type of luggage they carry.

A few Southern whites support the Republican Party. They are called "scalawags" by most white Southerners, who consider them traitors. But some are people of property and influence who opposed secession. They feel that the future of the South—as well as their own futures—lies with Northern interests. They are more interested in convincing Northern capitalists to invest in railroads, mines, cotton mills, and machine shops than they are in racial issues.

The Republican Party also receives strong support from independent white farmers who resent the political domination of white planters. They oppose the return of former Confederates to political power and will support black rights as long as blacks do not intrude on what they consider white territory.

Even as African-Americans make progress, President Johnson fails to support their efforts. Although Congress can now override his vetoes, Johnson still has considerable power to affect Reconstruction. As commander-in-chief of the army, he removes generals who are willing to carry out the orders of the Congress and replaces them with generals hostile to black rights. He removes Edwin Stanton from the cabinet despite a Congressional law, the Tenure of Office Act, forbidding him to do so. Stanton, who was appointed Secretary of War by Lincoln and remained in office after his assassination, was cooperating with the Republicans. His dismissal outrages Congress. In retaliation, the Republicans try to impeach the president but fail to reach the required two-thirds majority by one vote.

In the summer of 1868, the Republicans deny Johnson their party's nomination for president. Instead, they choose the commanding general of the army, Ulysses S. Grant, a popular Civil War hero. Grant has carried out the Reconstruction policies of Congress faithfully even though he is not particularly sympathetic to African-Americans.

While black voters in the South overwhelmingly support Grant, Southern whites in those states that have been readmitted to the Union (Arkansas, Louisiana, Georgia, Florida, Tennessee, and North and South Carolina) rally around the Democratic Party. They try to intimidate blacks to stop them from voting. Landlords evict tenants who dare to vote. A terrorist army, the Ku Klux Klan, is organized by former Confederate general Nathan Bedford Forrest, the commander of the troops who massacred hundreds of captured black soldiers at Fort Pillow. The Klan, along with other terrorist groups, systematically murders black politicians and political leaders throughout the South. Yet despite the Klan's efforts, blacks vote in large numbers, carrying the South for Grant. One newspaper reporter observes the determination of African-Americans to vote:

> *In defiance of fatigue, hardship, hunger, and threats of employers, blacks had come en masse to the polls. Without shoes, [wearing] patched clothing, they stood on line despite a storm waiting for the chance to vote. The hunger to have the same chances as the white men they feel and comprehend. . . .*

Harper's Weekly prints a drawing of two disguised Klan members in 1868.

To black people, the elections of 1868 establish the first American government to represent their interests. Black voters not only make a Republican presidential victory possible, they also vote some 600 black candidates into office. Some candidates are Northern and Southern blacks born in freedom who see in Reconstruction an opportunity to help their people and themselves. Many are ministers, while others are former slaves, some of whom served in the Union army. A few black candidates decide to make politics their career and are elected to be Congressional representatives, United States senators, lieutenant governors, state treasurers, superintendents of education, and state legislators. These black leaders include Robert Smalls in South Carolina, Blanche Bruce and P. B. S. Pinchback in Louisiana, and James Lynch in Mississippi. For the most part, however, blacks win low-level positions such as justices of the peace, sheriffs, councilmen, judges, aldermen, and school board members.

Congress tries to give additional support to black voters in 1869 by passing the Fifteenth Amendment, which prohibits federal and state governments from depriving any citizen of the vote on account of "race, color, or previous condition of servitude." But the amendment contains many weaknesses. It fails to make voting requirements universal, nor does it protect the rights of blacks to run for office and sit on juries. It also fails to prohibit literacy tests, poll taxes, and educational testing

Among black leaders of the period are Robert Smalls (left), a Civil War hero, who serves in the South Carolina House of Representatives and Senate, and in the U.S. Congress, and P. B. S. Pinchback who is elected to the U.S. Senate from Louisiana, but is never allowed to take his seat.

as requirements for voting. The amendment leaves the way open to deny blacks their voting rights on other grounds, such as lack of education and failure to pay special taxes. Eventually the South will use these loopholes to disfranchise both black and poor white voters.

As far as Congress is concerned, the Fifteenth Amendment means that their Reconstruction work is done. But black rights are far from secure. Even though Republicans control many state offices, they are regarded as aliens by most Southern whites. White Republicans find themselves in a bind. If they seek alliances with white Democrats, blacks turn against them. If they side with blacks, whites are hostile. Republicans are also plagued with other problems. They control a tremendous number of jobs, and blacks and whites struggle for those positions. For many Republicans, their livelihood depends upon politics. They make overtures to the Democrats by giving them jobs to defuse their hostility. This angers black Republicans, who feel that appeasing hostile whites is a waste of time.

Yet most state and local offices are won by whites. Whites control all legislatures except in South Carolina, where blacks gain control. The Democratic Party becomes known as the Party of Redemption, as its leaders pledge to "redeem" the South from the Republican combination of "carpetbaggers, scalawags, and niggers." In the 1870s, the "Bourbons," a group of Democrats, organize white resistance to black progress. The Bourbons—wealthy planters and merchants who control the party—are determined to restore white rule to the South and to modernize it, as long as modernization does not challenge their political and economic domination.

Between 1869 and 1871, the Ku Klux Klan acts as a military force, serving the interests of the Democratic Party, the planter class, and those who want white supremacy restored. Whites beat and murder thousands of blacks and their white supporters. While the first victims are the political and social leaders of the black community, whites murder blacks for almost any reason. A 103-year-old woman is whipped, as is a paralyzed man. Klansmen burn churches and schools, lynch teachers and educated blacks. Black landowners are driven off their property or murdered. Blacks are whipped for refusing to work for whites, for having intimate relations with whites, for arguing with whites, for having jobs whites want, for reading a newspaper or owning a book, or simply for being black.

A few state governments fight back. In Tennessee and Arkansas, Republicans organize a police force that arrests Klansmen and carries out executions. In Texas, Governor Edmund Davis organizes a

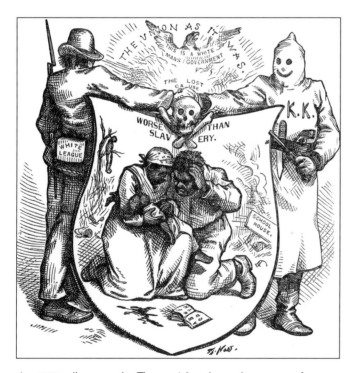

An 1870s illustration by Thomas Nast shows the situation for African-Americans as "worse than slavery," as they are victimized by both the Klan and the white power structure.

crack state police unit, with 40 percent of its officers black. The police make more than 6,000 arrests and stop the Klan. Sometimes individuals resist. Blacks lynch three whites in Arkansas who have murdered a black lawyer. Armed groups of blacks and whites fight Klansmen in North and South Carolina. But the price paid for resistance is heavy, and many states are helpless against Klan terror. In Colfax, Louisiana, when blacks try to defend their town against a white mob, 280 are massacred. President Grant condemns the slaughter in a letter to the Senate:

> *a butchery of citizens was committed at Colfax, which in blood-thirstiness and barbarity is hardly surpassed by any acts of savage warfare. . . . Insuperable obstructions were thrown in the way of punishing these murderers, and the so-called conservative papers of the state not only justified the massacre but denounced as federal tyranny and despotism the attempt of the United States officers to bring them to justice. . . .*

Between 1870 and 1871, Congress passes a series of Enforcement Acts—criminal codes that protect citizens' rights to vote, hold office, serve on juries, and receive equal protection of laws. If the states fail to act, the federal government may intervene.

President Grant responds by decreeing that "insurgents are in rebellion against the authority of the United States." Federal troops are sent to restore law and order in many areas where violence is raging. In nine counties of South Carolina, martial law is declared, and Klansmen are tried before predominantly black juries.

By 1873, with the violence under control, it seems that, with federal support, Reconstruction might possibly work. The question is whether it will have the chance to do so.

THREE

FROM RESTORATION TO "REDEMPTION" 1870–1880

IN 1874, T. McCANTS STEWART, a black man who left South Carolina to live in Boston, returns to visit his native state. He is ready to fight anyone who discriminates against him: "I put a chip on my shoulder and dared any man to knock it off." Stewart is astonished to find he is accepted wherever he goes.

> *I entered a dining room as bold as a lion. The whites at the table appeared not to have noted my presence. I can go into saloons and get refreshments even as in New York. I can stop in and drink a glass of soda and be more politely waited on than in New England.*

As Stewart travels he sees signs of progress. Blacks and whites attend the same theaters, ride the same streetcars, eat and drink in the same restaurants and saloons. The two races work and live side by side. Black politicians and white politicians sit in the same legislature. Working-class blacks and whites socialize in bars, brothels, gambling dens, and at sporting events. Stewart even sees a black policeman arrest a white man.

In South Carolina, blacks and their white allies pass bills to prohibit racial discrimination on railway lines, in theaters, hotels, courts, and juries; and in politics. They guarantee the right of all citizens to carry weapons and the right of people to work in whatever occupation they wish. The state legislature establishes public schools for all children and orphanages and hospitals for black people; medical treatment for the poor; penitentiaries; asylums and hospitals; and provides for legal counsel and protection of wives and children from abuse. African-Americans have their own churches, social clubs, and fraternal organizations.

After the Civil War, hundreds of white teachers and ministers come to the South to help educate newly freed men and women and their children.

Other travelers comment on similar progress in areas throughout the South. An editorial in the *Virginia Dispatch* notes: "Nobody here objects to sitting in political conventions with Negroes. Nobody here objects to serving on juries with Negroes. No lawyer objects to practicing in court with Negro lawyers present. And in both houses [of the legislature] Negroes are allowed to sit as they have a right to sit." Albert Morgan, a Yankee who works to gain education and political rights for blacks, reflects years later, "The period from 1869 to 1875 was one of substantial and . . . wonderful progress." Despite the real progress, civil rights laws are not generally enforced, and separation remains the most common mode of society.

The greatest area of progress is in education. Harriet Beecher Stowe, the author of *Uncle Tom's Cabin*, observes that blacks "cried for the spelling book as bread and pleaded for teachers as a necessity of life." Schools are built for both black students and white but, for the most part, are segregated. Only a few communities have integrated schools. In New Orleans, after a bitter fight, blacks and whites attend the same schools, but on the state level segregation rules. The University of South Carolina is integrated, which leads white students and faculty to withdraw. Other white students take their place, however, and get along well with blacks. Northern professors replace Southern.

While most Southern whites oppose the education of blacks, they realize that an attempt to dismantle the educational system will lead to a serious confrontation. In rural areas, where landowners have life-and-death power over their workers, many planters allow black children to attend rural schools only when their labor is not needed in the fields.

Some Southerners are aware of the significant gains blacks are making. Edward Allford Pollard, a Virginian who admits that he "always insisted on regarding the Negro specifically inferior to the white man—a lower order of human being who was indebted to what he had of civilization to the institution of slavery" confesses that "his former views of the Negro were wrong." Traveling through the South, Pollard finds that African-Americans are not the "degraded poor, intellectually helpless people" he thought they were. Instead he observes:

> that this singularly questionable creature has shown a capacity for education that has astonished . . . his former masters; that he has given proofs of good citizenship . . . that his condition has been on the whole that of progress . . . that

so far from being a stationary barbarian, the formerly despised black man promises to become a true follower of the highest civilization and . . . exemplary citizen of the South.

But black progress—made in the face of continuing white hostility—is soon challenged by larger economic forces. In 1873, a major economic depression causes the nation's economy to collapse. The effects are catastrophic in the South. The price of cotton drops 50 percent, causing independent white farmers to lose their lands. Blacks are hardest hit, both economically and politically. Many are worse off than ever before.

By 1873, Northerners refuse to continue their support of the collapsing Republican governments. Their interests are elsewhere. In the 1874 elections, Democrats gain a majority in the House of Representatives. With the Democrats' return to

Some black families manage to buy a piece of land and build a simple home on it and grow vegetables. By doing so, they can partially escape from the oppression of Jim Crow.

For many African-Americans, the end of the Civil War raises the hope of owning land. Most black farmers work for whites, but hundreds of thousands do manage to buy farms—a major accomplishment in the era of Jim Crow.

power, Reconstruction is in the hands of its enemies. White Republicans in the South seem unwilling to push Reconstruction further. They abandon their black supporters, whose votes put them in office, and appeal to white Democrats by supporting discriminatory legislation. In 1873, the United States Supreme Court joins the assault on black rights, ruling that the Fourteenth Amendment protects only their federal rights guaranteed by the Constitution. This means that most black rights now fall under state jurisdiction. Shortly afterward, the Court rules that the federal government has the power to punish only violations of rights by states—not by individuals. It is up to the states to punish individuals who violate black rights.

The shift of opinion in the North encourages Southern whites to start another reign of terror against black political power. Black Republicans are attacked by violent and unrepentant white Southerners whose goal is to "redeem" the South and restore white rule.

In 1875, Mississippi "redeems" itself from Republican rule by terror and murder. This strategy, called the Mississippi Plan, is applied ruthlessly throughout the state, using violence, economic intimidation, and fraud against black Republicans. White terrorists murder hundreds of teachers, church leaders, and local Republican organizers. One man brags they shoot blacks "just the same as birds." The state governor asks President Grant for help but Grant refuses to send troops. He complains, "The whole public are tired out with these . . . outbreaks in the South . . . and are ready now to condemn any interference on the part of the government." On election day, Mississippi's whites stuff or destroy ballot boxes, and drive away black voters. Democrats win in a landslide even though there are many more Republican voters.

By 1876, Democrats regain control of almost every Southern state. One exception is South Carolina, where Republican control seems secure, with a large majority of black voters. But whites, led by Martin W. Gary, set out to destroy the Republican Party with the same tactics used in Mississippi against blacks—terror and violence. Gary's plan is simple.

> *Every Democrat should control the vote of one Negro by intimidation, purchase, keeping him away, or as each individual shall determine. . . . argument has no effect of them [blacks]. They can only be influenced by their fears.*

On July 4, 1876 in Hamburg, South Carolina, an armed confrontation occurs between a mob of whites and a black militia group. The blacks, outnumbered and outgunned, surrender. Five black soldiers are executed.

The Hamburg massacre triggers more violence. Democrats murder, whip, and terrorize Republicans—both black and white—throughout the state. On election day, men travel from Georgia and North Carolina to vote the Democratic ticket, some as many as twenty times. Although blacks have a 20,000 majority in the state, the Democrats declare themselves winners in a close race. The Republican governor, John Chamberlain, refuses to accept the results and claims victory. The same thing happens in Louisiana: Democrats and Republicans both claim the governorship. The parties in both states turn to the president of the United States to resolve their disputes.

However, no one is sure who is president. At first the Democratic Party seems to have won the presidential election. Its candidate, Samuel Tilden, has a majority of more than 250,000 votes and a total of 184 electoral votes. He is one vote short of the majority necessary to be elected president. His Republican opponent, Rutherford B. Hayes, has 166 electoral votes. But the votes of Florida, along with those of South Carolina and Louisiana, are in doubt. Together, they have 19 electoral votes. Democrats and Republicans in South Carolina and Louisiana each claim to have won the governor's office and two sets of returns are presented to Congress. For a moment, there are fears of a new civil war. Hayes is declared president by a special election committee (which the Republicans control), but many Democrats are outraged. They threaten to refuse to confirm Hayes as president. At this critical moment the Southern Democrats make a deal with the Republicans. They will support Hayes if he promises to withdraw federal troops from the South and to let whites control their own states. This means that Hayes must also support Democratic claims for governor in Louisiana and South Carolina. As one Southern newspaper reports: "It matters little to us who rules in Washington, if South Carolina is allowed to have Hampton and Home Rule." Hayes also agrees to appoint at least one Southerner to the cabinet and to give Southerners control over federal appointments in their sections.

The North's idealistic war aims—to free and protect African-Americans—are no longer a priority. The New York *Herald Tribune* expresses the feeling of most Northerners when it states that Negroes—after "ample opportunities to develop their own latent capabilities"—have succeeded only in proving that "as a race they are idle, ignorant and vicious." South Carolina's new Democratic governor, Wade Hampton, makes it clear who must rule in the South: The lesson that the white people learned is that no Negro must ever again be allowed to gain an ascendancy in politics.

As soon as Rutherford B. Hayes takes office, he keeps his promise to the South. In March 1877, he withdraws the last detachment of federal troops stationed in New Orleans. Frederick Douglass, the great black abolitionist leader and a strong supporter of the Republican Party and black suffrage, denounces the Republican betrayal of his people:

President Rutherford B. Hayes

You have emancipated us, and I thank you for it. You have enfranchised us, and I thank you for it. But what is your emancipation, what is your enfranchisement if the black man, having been made free by the letter of the law, is unable to exercise that freedom? You have turned us loose to the sky, the whirlwind, and worst of all to our infuriated masters. What does it all amount to if the black man having been freed from the slaveholder's lash is to be made subject to the slaveholder's shotgun?

Southern politicians promise Hayes they will protect black rights but instead set out to undo the work of Reconstruction and gain control of the South. Schools, hospitals, penitentiaries and other public institutions that had been created for poor whites and for blacks are closed. New laws restrict the freedom of black labor and give planters increased power over workers.

Black voters in most states are systematically eliminated unless they vote Democratic. White Republicans, many of whom had been elected with black votes, abandon their black supporters. But even though a number of black Republicans manage to hold on to their offices, their independence and influence are gone.

The restoration of white supremacy to the South leads some black grassroots organizers such as Henry Adams to call for a mass exodus of African-Americans to find better lives and protest the denial of their constitutional rights. Adams escaped from slavery before the Civil War, fought against the South in the Union army, and then became a Republican Party organizer in Louisiana. Beginning in the mid-1870s, he documents the increasing violence and oppression in rural Louisiana. By

1877, Adams concludes there will be no justice for Southern blacks. It is time for them to leave the South.

> *So long as the white men of the South are going to kill us, there was no way that we could better our condition there. We said that the whole South had gotten into the very hands that held us as slaves. We felt we had almost been slaves under these men. Then we said there was no hope for us and we better go.*

In Tennessee, an elderly farmer by the name of Benjamin "Pap" Singleton is also encouraging groups to move to Kansas. Land is cheap there and the state governor invites blacks to settle. Tens of thousands of Southern black farmers and sharecroppers leave their homes and head for Kansas. They are not simply fleeing oppression. Deep spiritual forces drive them as well. Many African-Americans believe the time has come for God to lead them out of the South as he once led the children of Israel out of Egypt. The great abolitionist Sojourner Truth voices this vision of her people:

> *I have prayed so long that my people would go to Kansas and that God would make straight the way before them. I believe as much in that move as I do in the moving of the children of Egypt going out to Canaan. This colored people is going to be a people. Do you think God has them robbed and scourged all the days of their life for nothing?*

The journey is filled with heartbreak. Thousands of families leave in covered wagons or on foot. Many fail to take sufficient provisions for the journey, trusting that God will provide. Steamboat captains often refuse to take them upriver. Some planters pursue and murder them. When groups of destitute migrants reach St. Louis, they find no relief and no free transportation to Kansas. Many return home.

As bad as political conditions are for Southern blacks, economic conditions are worse. Blacks want their own land, but Southern whites fear that if blacks own land they will no longer be willing to work for them. For Southern whites, land is the source of their wealth. Cotton is a "money crop," which can yield fortunes when the price is high. To plant, tend, and harvest a cotton crop, whites need a cheap labor force. Denied land, most black farmers—and many poor whites—have no choice

"The Fugitive's Song" is dedicated to the black abolitionist and orator, Frederick Douglass, "a graduate from the 'peculiar institution'" of slavery, and shows him as a young man escaping bondage.

but to become sharecroppers. They work a planter's land in exchange for a share of the proceeds after it is sold. Because sharecroppers receive no money until the crop is sold, they must live on credit from the local merchant to buy the clothes, food, seed, and tools they need through the year. As the sharecroppers make purchases, the costs, plus interest, are deducted from their share of the crop. When the crop is sold, the planter takes a share, and whatever is left goes to the "croppers."

Under an honest system, sharecroppers might earn some money in a good year. But many merchants and landlords overcharge farmers for supplies. In one store, black tenants pay twelve and a half cents a pound for meat, when it costs six-and-a-half cents elsewhere. Black farmers pay $7.50 a barrel for flour when the normal price

The migration to Kansas

is $4.50. On top of the markup, the stores' interest charges range from 30 to 300 percent.

What's more, some landlords and merchants cheat. If the sharecroppers dispute their figures, they may trigger the planters' anger. Ned Cobb, a farmer in Alabama, sees what happens to a neighbor, Henry Kirkland, when he objects to a landlord's accounting:

[Emmet], the youngest boy of Kirkland, was keeping an account of everything that his daddy got from Clay. . . . Mr. Clay [the landlord] flew into a passion over that book business and threw his pistol on Henry and deadened him right there. When he killed the old man, he shot Emmet right through the lung, but Emmet got over it. They put Mr. Clay in jail, but he didn't stay there long. He was a big farmer, and they got him out.

By 1880, it is clear that African-Americans will be left to the mercy of Southern whites. One African-American comments: "The whole South—every state in the South—has got into the very hands of men that held us as slaves."

FOUR

EDUCATION: A ROAD TO FREEDOM

FOR ADDIE AND JERRY HOLTZCLAW, the South is home. In the 1880s, the Holtzclaws become tenant farmers in Virginia, renting a farm instead of working as sharecroppers. They are free to run their farm any way they want, as long as they pay the rent at the end of the year.

Misfortune plagues them from the start. Within months, one ox has a broken neck, and the mule dies from a strange disease. Their last hope to meet their debts is their corn crop. By August, the corn is golden yellow and ready for picking.

Early one Saturday morning, the Holtzclaws harvest the ripened corn. All through the day, they pull the ears from their stalks and lay them in piles across the field. By evening, the corn is all picked. In the morning, storm clouds appear, but Addie Holtzclaw refuses to allow her family to gather the crop. "Sunday is the Lord's day and must be kept holy," she says. While the Holtzclaws are at church, a torrential rainstorm pours down. The family rushes home in time to see their corn crop floating down the Chattahoochee River, carrying away their dream of freedom.

Jerry and Addie Holtzclaw return to sharecropping. Despite their tragedy, they are determined that their children will have better lives. The only way to achieve this is through education. Because there is no school in Roanoke, the Holtzclaws, with other sharecroppers, build a rough school with no floors or chimney. They hire a teacher. The major problem is their landlord, as William Holtzclaw later describes:

The landlord wanted us to pick cotton. But Mother wanted me to remain in school. So she used to outgeneral him by hiding me behind skillets, ovens, and pots. Then she would slip me to school the back way, pushing me through the woods and underbrush, until it was safe for me to travel alone. Whereupon she would return to the plantation and try to make up for the landlord for the work of us in the cotton field.

While most African-Americans appreciate Northern assistance, they also want to take control of their own schools and provide black teachers as role models for children.

When he can no longer hide from the landlord, his mother devises a new scheme. He and his brother go to school on alternate days, and each teaches the other what he misses.

The Holtzclaws' experience is repeated throughout the South. Hundreds of thousands of children attend country schools. Churches organize "Sabbath schools," where children learn to read, write, and spell. Benjamin Mays, another sharecropper's son, never forgets the support he receives the day he makes a recitation to the congregation of his Sabbath school.

After my recitation, the house went wild. Old women waved their handkerchiefs, old men stomped their feet, and the people applauded long and loud. It was a terrific experience for a nine-year-old boy. There were predictions I would go places in life. The people in the church did not contribute one dime to help me with my education. But they gave me something far more valuable. They gave me encouragement, the thing I most needed. They expressed such confidence in me that I always felt that I could never betray their trust, never let them down.

But many rural schools can provide only a limited education. When William Holtzclaw reaches adulthood and is ready to work in the fields, his father offers to release his son from that obligation if he will continue his education. William immediately writes a letter to Booker T. Washington, the black educator, at the Tuskegee Institute in Alabama.

Dear book. I wants to go to Tuskegee to get an ejercashun. Can I come?

He sends this letter to "Book Washington" with no address. Somehow the letter finds its way. "Come," Washington replies.

Booker T. Washington is a man with a mission: to uplift the rural poor through education, as he uplifted himself. Born in slavery, Washington was warned by his mother that reading was dangerous for slaves. Yet, like many newly freed African-Americans, Washington was determined to learn no matter what the risk.

Washington made his way to Hampton Institute in Virginia, where he received the education that shaped his thinking. Hampton was the creation of General Samuel Armstrong, a white Northern Civil War general, who believed that African-Americans should be subordinate to whites. Hampton paid little attention to academic training. Most students learned what was then called industrial skills—how to plant, take care of cattle, do carpentry and domestic work . . . tasks that prepared them for future employment, but also condemned them to lives of menial labor.

Booker T. Washington is the most respected black leader in America in the late nineteenth and early twentieth centuries. Crowds come from great distances to hear him speak.

When Booker T. Washington graduates from Hampton, he is recommended by General Armstrong to take over a school in Tuskegee, Alabama. Washington makes the most of this opportunity. He transforms Tuskegee from a run-down rural school into an institute for training teachers. Washington's dream is to produce educators who will train rural children for manual and domestic labor. Courses in reading, writing, spelling, and math are limited to the basics, as Washington does not believe in classical education. Male students learn practical skills such as farming, animal care, mechanical skills, and brick making, while women learn domestic skills. Great emphasis is placed on cleanliness and personal hygiene. Washington wants his students to learn to appreciate the joy of work.

My plan was to have them taught the best methods of labor in order for them to see not only the utility of labor but its beauty and dignity. They would be taught how to lift labor up from drudgery and toil and would learn to love work for its own sake.

Washington is able to cooperate with whites and convert potential opponents in Tuskegee into supporters. He reassures them that his students will not be educated beyond their station. Washington is opposed to African-Americans becoming involved in politics and competing for jobs with working-class whites.

Tuskegee is a great success. A new generation of teachers graduate and spread their learning throughout the rural South. William Holtzclaw, the sharecropper's son, eventually founds Utica College in Mississippi, basing it on the Tuskegee model. The Tuskegee–Hampton philosophy of education soon begins to receive financial support from Northern foundations.

An increasing number of young black women become teachers—the only profession open to them. They teach children everything from baking cakes and canning peaches to reading, writing, arithmetic, history, and geography. They instill race

For many rural black children, the only school—when there is one—is a one-room schoolhouse, often built by their parents.

pride in their students. To compensate for the lack of books, maps, writing paper, pencils, and pens, which many white-controlled school boards deny black children, black teachers use their ingenuity to raise funds. They mobilize local communities to buy supplies, construct buildings and furniture, and provide food for needy students.

The task of educating the race is made more difficult by white resistance, especially in the rural South, which depends on child labor. One white planter states the opinion of many when he comments:

Education is the worst thing for niggers. It spoils them for the fields. Gives them airs. Makes them insolent and disrespectful. What's the point of teaching them something that they ain't never gonna use? Only makes them restless.

Most black parents cannot afford to send their children to school. Many families need their children to work with them in the fields. Even when children receive a good education, they rarely find jobs equal to their training. Some black parents begin to lose faith in the ability of education alone to change the status of African-Americans:

Once I was a great believer in Negro education, but now I doubt whether it's good or not. You educate your children, then [what are you] gonna do? You got jobs for them? You got any business for them to go into? What's the use of becoming a bookkeeper if you got no books to keep?

With little chance to get an education or to own land in the rural South, a growing number of African-American men and women, many of them young, try to escape the grinding poverty, monotony, and hopelessness of rural life. They drift into the cities of the South. They hope to start new lives there and escape the racism of the rural South.

FIVE

Jim Crow Comes to Town

IN 1883, IDA B. WELLS, a young black schoolteacher in Memphis, Tennessee, is quietly traveling in a first-class railroad car, for which she has bought a ticket, when the conductor rudely tells her that she has to move to the "colored car."

I refused, saying the forward car was a smoker, and as I was in the ladies' car, I proposed to stay. He tried to drag me out of my seat, but the moment he caught hold of my arm, I fastened my teeth on the back of his hand.

Finally forced to leave the train, Ida B. Wells sues and wins. When the decision is then reversed by a higher court, she is devastated.

I had firmly believed all along that the law was on our side and would give us justice. I feel shorn of that belief and utterly discouraged. If it were possible, I would gather the race in my arms and fly away with them. God, is there no redress, no peace nor justice for us? Teach us what to do, for I am sorely, bitterly disgusted.

The incident alerts Ida B. Wells to a new danger to herself and her people. Jim Crow—legalized segregation—has come to the cities of the South.

An illustrator of the Reconstruction period shows a scene of a black woman forced to leave a first-class railroad car—modeled on the experience of Ida B. Wells.

The move toward legal segregation is fostered by the profound economic changes taking place in the cities of the South. An industrial boom is triggered by the arrival of the railroad and by an influx of Northern capital. The new industries attract thousands of rural whites and blacks to the cities. For the arriving black men, the only work available is in low-paying jobs on railroads and levees, and as teamsters, hod carriers, porters, and waiters. Because these jobs are hard and dirty, and the pay low, whites usually avoid them. For African-American women, most jobs are closed. However, there is a large demand for black women as cooks, maids, and washerwomen for white families. The pay is low, the hours long, and many women suffer sexual harassment from the white men of the household. One woman writes:

For more than thirty years, or since I was ten years old, I have been a servant in white families. I frequently work from fourteen to sixteen hours a day. I am allowed to go home to my children only once in two weeks. Even then I am not permitted to stay all night. I not only have to nurse a little white child, I have to wash and act as playmate to three other children. And what do I get for this work. The pitiful sum of $10 a month! With this money I'm expected to pay my house rent, which is four dollars a month, and to feed and clothe myself and three children.

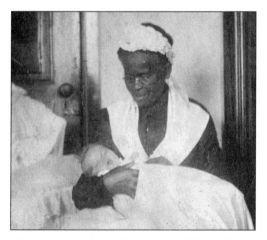

Almost 90 percent of the jobs available for black women outside of farm work are in domestic work. The women work long hours for meals and small salaries.

As blacks and whites compete for jobs, whites increasingly demand segregation. The first generation of African-Americans born in freedom have no intention of playing the role of the slave. The editor of the Fisk college newspaper announces the arrival of what many call the New Negro: "We are not the Negro from whom the chains of slavery fell a quarter of a century ago, most assuredly not. We are now qualified as being the equal of whites, and should be treated as such."

Whites confess they are frightened and puzzled by the New Negro. One white man writes to a newspaper: "The younger generation of Negroes [has] lost that wholesome respect for white men, without which the two races, one inferior, cannot live in peace and harmony together."

Reacting to their fears, whites start imposing Jim Crow laws to segregate the races. The term "Jim Crow" comes into being in the early nineteenth century, when a white minstrel by the name of Thomas "Daddy" Rice entertains audiences by blacking his face, dressing in beggar's rags, and singing a song called "Jump Jim Crow." Rice dances and jumps around onstage in a stereotyped and racist caricature of a black person. Rice's performance is highly popular. Soon the term Jim Crow is part of the American vocabulary. In the 1840s, antislavery newspapers use the term to describe separate railroad cars for blacks and whites in the North. By the late nineteenth century, the term is used to describe the rigidly enforced laws and customs that achieve separation of the races in the South.

While segregation begins spreading through the South after the Civil War, it is not yet formalized. In some cities, blacks and whites ride the same streetcars, eat in the same restaurants, drink in the same bars, and attend the same theaters. In other cities, this mingling is prohibited. However, as white fear and resentment increase, a uniformity begins to appear throughout the region. In Memphis, parks that had been open to both races are now closed to blacks. Theaters that allowed blacks to sit among whites now segregate them. Black passengers are prohibited from traveling in first-class railroad cars with whites even if they have purchased first-class tickets.

Many blacks, like Ida B. Wells, find the Jim Crow laws on public transportation troubling. On trains, African-American men and women are forced to sit in a segregated "smoking" car, where men of both races drink, smoke, and sometimes fight. W. E. B. Du Bois, a student at Fisk University in Tennessee at this time, describes a car he rode in:

By the early twentieth century segregation is seen in almost every area of public life in the South. Banks have separate rooms for black customers and for white customers.

The "Jim-Crow" car is next to the baggage car and engine. The car is caked with dirt, the floor is gummy and the windows dirty. The conductor gruffly asks for your tickets. Lunch rooms either "don't serve niggers" or serve them at some dirty and ill-attended hole-in-the-wall. Toilet rooms are often filthy.

In 1887, Wells begins to write for a local black newspaper, *The Free Speech and Headlight.* When she publicly criticizes the white community for the poor quality of education for black children, Wells loses her teaching job. She becomes a full-time journalist and continues her attack on discrimination. She urges blacks to defend themselves against the increasing number of lynchings—the murder of blacks by mobs.

Not until the Negro rises in his might and takes a hand in resenting . . . cold-blooded murders, if he has to burn up whole towns, will a halt be called to wholesale lynching. When the white man knows he runs as great a risk as biting the dust every time his Afro-American victim does, he will have a greater respect for Afro-American life.

In 1892, white violence strikes close to home for Wells. A good friend, Thomas Moss, opens a grocery store in competition with a nearby white-owned store. The white owner hires a group of off-duty deputy sheriffs to raid Moss's store and destroy it. Moss and two friends, not knowing the raiders are law enforcement officials, defend his store and wound several men. They are imprisoned. Several days after their arrest, masked vigilantes drag the three men from their cells, take them to a deserted railroad yard, and shoot them to death.

Enraged by her friend's death, Wells writes passionate editorials, attacking the Memphis police for failing to prevent the lynching or arrest the known killers. Blacks protest by boycotting white stores and streetcar lines.

Many blacks are arrested and falsely charged with vagrancy so that they can be sent to chain gangs and forced to work on county roads or for private contractors.

The lynchings are a turning point in the journalist's life.

I had accepted the idea that although lynching was . . . unreasoning anger over the terrible crime of rape . . . perhaps the mob was justified in taking [a rapist's] life. But then Thomas Moss, Calvin McDowell, and Henry Stewart had been lynched in Memphis, and they had committed no crime against a white woman. This is what opened my eyes to what lynching really was—an excuse to get rid of Negroes who were acquiring wealth and property and thus keep the race terrorized and "keep the niggers down."

The journalist Ida B. Wells

Ida B. Wells investigates more than 700 lynchings and finds that many victims are lynched not for rape, but for "insubordination," or making threats, or for having sex with white women who are willing partners.

The suggestion that white women would willingly have sexual relations with black men angers white Memphis. A mob destroys *The Free Speech* while Wells is out of town and then threatens to lynch her if she returns. Forced into exile in the North, Wells launches a national crusade against lynching that captures attention from the nation and from Europe. Almost single-handedly, she prepares the groundwork for what will become a major campaign against lynching in the twentieth century. She urges the black people of Memphis to leave the city: "There is nothing we can do about the lynchings now as we are outnumbered and without arms. Therefore there is only one thing left for us to do—save our money and leave town."

SIX

DISFRANCHISEMENT

IN 1887, A TRAIN TRAVELING between Memphis, Tennessee, and Vicksburg, Mississippi, comes to an unexpected stop at an isolated spot midway between the cities. Two men step down and enter the swampy wilderness. One is a white surveyor. The other is an imposing black man in the prime of life. He is Isaiah Montgomery, a successful black businessman who grew up in slavery. His dream is to build a utopia for black people in this wilderness, a place where black farmers will own their own land and businesses and run their own government. He calls his colony Mound Bayou after discovering Indian burial mounds on his property.

Using axes and dynamite, a small group of families begin to transform the wilderness into farmland. By 1900, a town has been built, with churches, schools, a post office, and a number of businesses. Cotton farms surround the town.

Montgomery insists that all children in the town go to school nine months of the year, almost twice as long as most black children attend school in the rest of the

The support of black churches helps many African-Americans survive the worst excesses of Jim Crow. The scene here is a baptismal ceremony of the 1890s.

rural South. Ben Green, who once was a student there, never forgets the impact the town makes on him:

> *For the children of Mound Bayou, the community was a source of pride.*
> *Everything here was Negro, from the symbols of law and authority and the man*
> *who ran the bank to the fellow [who] drove the road scraper. That gave us kids*
> *a sense of security and pride that colored kids didn't get elsewhere.*

But if Mound Bayou is an oasis in a desert, it is still not free from the surrounding world of whites. It exists because whites allow it to and because Montgomery makes sure to keep on good terms with powerful white planters and politicians.

In 1890, the African-American vote is eliminated in Mississippi, after poor whites and the conservative elite join forces to restrict black voting rights. Even though blacks are now deprived of much of their political power, more than 100,000 blacks still vote in the state. The state legislature calls a constitutional convention to legally disfranchise blacks. To ensure that the United States Supreme Court will not overturn the new law they write, no reference is made to color. It states that all voters must pay a poll tax and pass a literacy test. But James Vardaman, a rising Mississippi politician, makes the real purpose clear: "Mississippi's constitutional convention was held for no other purpose than to eliminate the nigger from politics; not the ignorant but the nigger."

The only black delegate allowed to attend the convention is Isaiah Montgomery. He agrees to speak in favor of disfranchisement if whites will end violence against blacks. He tells the delegates:

> *I have stood by, consenting and assisting to strike down the liberties of 123,000 free men. It is a fearful sacrifice laid upon the burning altar of liberty. I only ask that the laws be fairly applied, that the race problem be resolved, and that issues be discussed on some other basis than color line. What answer? Is our sacrifice accepted? Shall the great question be settled?*

The Mississippi legislators applaud Montgomery, but other blacks criticize him. Frederick Douglass is one of his harshest critics.

> *His address is a positive disaster to the race. He has been taken in by lying whites. No more flippant fool could have inflicted such a wound in our cause as Mr. Montgomery has.*

The racial peace that Montgomery dreams of is not to be. In Mississippi, prosperous blacks are driven out of their communities. Montgomery receives a letter from one prosperous friend asking for help.

Reverend Buchanan was banished from West Point. Whites thought his elegant mode of living had a bad effect on cooks and washerwomen who aspired to do likewise and became less disposed to work for whites. He was ordered to sell his business and remove his family under penalty of death.

Years later, Montgomery confesses that he made a serious mistake. He confides to Booker T. Washington: "I am coming to the conclusion that only federal intervention can bring democracy to America. The dominant race is seeking a retrogression of the Negro back to serfdom and slavery."

In the 1890s, as Mound Bayou prospers as an all-black community, farmers of both races begin to cooperate out of common need. Prices for their crops are low, interests rates are high, and Democratic politicians are indifferent to their suffering. As a result, Southern and Midwestern farmers organize a movement known as Populism. The Populists soon decide to nominate their own candidates for office.

While white farmers and black farmers cooperate on economic issues, they often divide on racial matters. Many white farmers are still troubled about the possibility of social equality between the races. But black farmers have other concerns. As one black farmer tells a white audience:

We don't want to rule the government; we don't want to come into your family; we don't want to enter your school house. We want equal rights at the ballot box and equal justice before the law; we want better wages for our labor and better prices for our produce; we want to lift the mortgage from the old cow and mule, which they have carried until they are sway-backed; we want to school our child, and we want a chance to earn our home.

Black organizers often risk their lives. In 1889, Oliver Cromwell travels to the back country of Leflore County, Mississippi, to organize a boycott of local white merchants and to begin a farmers' cooperative. The state militia violently suppresses the boycott. J. C. Engle, a textile merchant from New York, witnesses the action.

> *Negroes were shot down like dogs. Members of the posse not only killed people in the swamps but invaded homes and murdered men, women and children. A sixteen-year-old white boy beat the brains out of a little colored girl while a bigger brother with a gun kept the little one's parents off.*

Some white Populists encourage black–white political unity. Tom Watson, a Georgia Democrat turned Populist, is a United States congressman who defies his party to work for his state's farmers. While against social equality, he favors political equality. He tells an audience of both black and white farmers:

A Populist poster of the late nineteenth century

You are made to hate each other because on that hatred is rested the keystone of the arch of financial despotism which enslaves you both. You are deceived and blinded because you do not see how this race antagonism perpetuates a monetary system that beggars you both. . . . the colored tenant is in the same boat as the white tenant, the colored laborer with the white laborer, and that the accident of color can make no difference in the interests of farmers, croppers, and laborers. If you stand shoulder to shoulder with us in this fight, the People's party will wipe out the color line and put every man on his citizenship irrespective of color.

Other white Populists, such as Cyclone Davis, express great hostility toward blacks.

The worst sight of social equality to be seen in this land is the sight of a sweet white girl hoeing cotton in one row and a burley negro in the next. Talk of social equality when your industrial system forces a good woman's Anglo-Saxon girl down on a level with a burley negro in a cotton row. Oh my God! and this in a free America!

Statements like these convince many African-Americans that there has been no fundamental change in the hearts of white farmers. H. H. Styles, a black leader, points out:

I am afraid the Populists will eventually ruin my people. They remind them of the wrongs done them and promise to correct them. But they do not tell them that they were in the front ranks when that army of oppression came against the negro.

Although the Populists win some elections in the early 1890s, they are cheated out of others. The black vote is divided, with many farmers supporting the Populists, especially in Georgia and Texas. Urban blacks, however, tend to support the Democrats because "they trust them more." Democrats are also able to deliver many votes of sharecroppers, who depend upon them economically.

The rise of Populism takes place during the worst depression of the nineteenth century, which devastates the rural South. The turmoil caused by the elections and the economic crisis has grave consequences for blacks, who become targets of white frustration and fury. Segregation and disfranchisement laws multiply. Violence dramatically rises. Between 1889 and 1914 an epidemic of lynching breaks out, and more than 1,500 people are murdered. Southerners argue that the white man must lynch because black men rape. Actually lynching serves to restrict black economic independence and to police the

By the end of the nineteenth century, Southern whites are lynching more than a hundred blacks a year, with most never proven guilty of any crime. Here two black men have been lynched by a Florida mob.

color line in the South. The fact that as many as half of the black people lynched may be innocent bothers few whites. Fanny Preston, a white woman from Texas, expresses the general feeling of most whites when she comments, "It is better to lynch a few innocent blacks than to leave white women terrorized."

In Georgia, a man believed to be Edward Claus is lynched for allegedly assaulting Susie Johnson, a young schoolteacher. He is tied to a tree and shot to pieces by

The rural South is hit hard by the depression of the late nineteenth century. An old engraving shows a wandering freedman waiting for farm work.

the mob as the teacher looks on. Before he dies, he swears he is not Edward Claus and asks for time to prove it. The mob refuses and kills him. Several days later, the real Claus is caught, and the mob then lynches him. In Texas, a woman claims she was raped by a light-skinned black man, but a mob lynches a black man with very dark skin. In Arkansas, a black man is lynched for writing a sexually suggestive note to a white woman, even though he cannot read or write.

Out of the approximately 5,000 blacks lynched between 1880 and 1960, it is estimated that rape was the issue less than 35 percent of the time. The truth is that blacks are lynched for a variety of reasons—or for no reason at all. Men, women, and even children are lynched for bumping into somebody accidentally, arguing over a bill, making an innocent remark, not being properly servile, protecting their wives or daughters, not yielding the right of way, having an argument—or just being in the wrong place at the wrong time. In Palestine, Texas, a mob of whites goes on a rampage, hunting down and killing twenty blacks. The local sheriff cannot explain why:

Men were going about and killing Negroes as fast as they could find them, and so far as I have been able to ascertain, without any real cause at all. These Negroes had never done anything that I could discover. There was just a hot-headed gang hunting them down and killing them.

Many African-Americans leave the land for migrant jobs, such as work in turpentine forests and sawmills, and on levees and railroads.

The common belief is that lynch mobs are composed of the poorest and lowest members of the society. Yet senators, congressmen, judges, lawyers, doctors, teachers, planters, and merchants are often members of lynch mobs, or applaud their actions. Most sheriffs do not resist a mob coming to take a prisoner. Many sheriffs and jailers cooperate with the lynchers.

Occasionally whites protest lynching, especially if, in their judgment, it is without cause or particularly brutal. A group of Confederate veterans, while not condemning lynching, issues a statement against burning victims to death:

As Confederate veterans and law abiding citizens of Mississippi . . . we are vehemently and eternally opposed to the practice of burning a human being for any crime whatsoever. We appeal to all Confederate veterans . . . to help put a stop to this barbaric, unlawful, inhuman and ungodly crime of burning human beings.

Some blacks advocate resistance. Joseph Dalton of Alabama comments: "Lynching will stop down here if every time a Negro is chased by white hoodlums, he would turn around and get just one." In Texas, when a lynch mob storms a man's house, they encounter fierce resistance from a group of businessmen meeting there. Eleven members of the mob are killed. But resistance is dangerous. One white planter warns what can happen to militant blacks: "When a nigger gets ideas, the best thing is to get him underground as quick as possible."

As lynchings, segregation, and disfranchisement poison the air for the black community in almost every Southern state, Booker T. Washington, then relatively unknown as the head of Tuskegee Institute, is invited to address a segregated audience of blacks and influential whites at the Atlanta Cotton Exposition of 1895. The cotton exposition has been organized to promote the South's economy to Northern investors. One highlight is the Negro Building which contains exhibits that demonstrate the scientific, cultural, and mechanical achievements of African-Americans since slavery.

Washington sees his invitation to speak at the exhibition as a sign of white sympathy for his people's plight. He plans to deliver a speech that he hopes will solve the race problem and end the violence against his people. He overlooks the fact that many African-Americans in Atlanta are protesting against the exhibition.

As Washington mounts the speaker's platform, the mood of the crowd becomes hostile. People ask, "What's that nigger doing on the stage?" But when Washington begins his speech, criticizing his own people for seeking political power and for being too ambitious too soon, the crowd becomes attentive:

Our greatest danger is that in the great leap from slavery to freedom, we may overlook the fact that the masses of us are to live by the productions of our hands and fail to keep in our mind that we shall prosper as we learn to dignify and glorify common labor. It is at the bottom of life we should begin, at the

Lynchings by Klan groups or by mobs occur in nearly every Southern state.

bottom and not at the top. The opportunity to earn a dollar in a factory just now is worth infinitely more than to spend a dollar in an opera house."

Washington accepts the right of whites to impose political and legal restrictions on blacks. He warns blacks of the folly of seeking social equality:

The wisest of my race understand the agitation of questions of social equality is the extremist folly, and that progress in the enjoyment of all the privileges that will come to us must be the result of severe and constant struggle rather than of artificial forcing. . . . In all things that are purely social we can be as separate as fingers, yet one as the hand in all things essential to mutual progress.

The crowd roars its approval. Across the nation, the white press unanimously applauds his speech. Former abolitionists, railroad tycoons, and political leaders, including President Grover Cleveland, wire their congratulations. Many whites and blacks feel a new era of race relations has begun. But some blacks, such as John Hope, president of Atlanta University, refuse to accept Washington's compromise:

If we are not striving for equality, in heaven's name for what are we living? I regard it as cowardly and dishonest for any of our colored men to tell white people or colored people we are not striving for equality. Rise brothers! Be discontented. Let your discontent break mountain high against the wall of prejudice and swamp it to the very foundation. Then we shall not have to plead for justice nor on bended knee ask for mercy: for we shall be men.

One year after Washington's speech at the Cotton Exhibition, the Supreme Court hands down its decision in a landmark case, *Plessy v. Ferguson*. The case involves Homére Plessy, a black man in New Orleans, who challenges Louisiana's right to segregate the city's streetcars. The Court rules that a state can segregate the races as long as equal facilities are provided for both races. It is doubtful that anyone—including the justices of the Supreme Court—expects that both races will receive equal treatment. Jim Crow now has the blessing of the most powerful judicial body in the United States. In 1898, in *Williams v. Mississippi*, the Supreme Court also gives its blessing to disfranchisement by allowing states to use the poll tax and literacy tests to disqualify black voters. The message sent to African-Americans by whites is clear—there is no place for them in American society.

SEVEN

The Darkest Time

AS JIM CROW LAWS spread like a plague through the South, one state seems relatively immune. For many middle-class blacks, at least, North Carolina is a haven, lacking the harsh racial laws that characterize other Southern states. The Charlotte *Observer*, a black newspaper, praises the white community for its racial moderation:

> *North Carolina's white people are progressive people. Afro Americans in no other state enjoy such freedom and free speech.*

In the port city of Wilmington, located on the Eastern Seaboard, the African-American community prides itself on its progress. David Fuller, a black writer, comments on the harmonious racial relations.

> *The best feeling among the races prevailed in Wilmington. The negro and his white brother walked their beats on the police force; white and black commit-*

*teemen sat together . . . white and black mechanics worked together; white
and black teachers in the same schools.*

In Wilmington, the middle-class black community prospers. Many African-Americans own their own small businesses or property, or hold good jobs. They have created strong social and fraternal clubs that present cultural events, concerts, poetry readings, and debates, and offer social services to the needy. Church and the family are the twin pillars supporting the black community.

Blacks not only prosper economically in North Carolina, but they also achieve political power. Although most African-Americans continue to support the Republican Party, they join forces with North Carolina's Populist movement. White Populists, most of whom are farmers, rebel against the Democrats, who have controlled the state since the end of Reconstruction. The coalition of Populists and Republicans results in stunning political victories in 1894 and 1896. As a result, African-Americans hold a significant number of state and city offices, and win a Congressional seat. As the election campaign of 1898 begins, African-Americans seem confident they can hold on to their gains, if not improve upon them.

But beneath the seemingly harmonious race relations, Judge Robert Winston sees violent passions emerging in the white community.

*The great body of whites and blacks were drifting apart. The breach between the
races widens. The animosity is intense, but it is repressed and silent, revealing itself in violent lynchings, mobs, and crusades that eliminate all opposition.*

The leaders of the Democratic Party resolve to regain political control by any and all means—legal and illegal. They launch a vicious attack on African-Americans to split the coalition between them and white Populists. They charge that blacks seek political power in order to have sexual access to white women. The Wilmington *Messenger*, a white newspaper, publishes an inflammatory speech by

The North Carolina press stirs up fears in the white community by publishing false and racist articles.

Georgia white supremacist Rebecca Felton calling for violence against blacks as a defense against rape.

> *If it requires lynching to protect woman's dearest possession from ravening, drunken human beasts, then I say lynch a thousand negroes a week, if it is necessary.*

Alex Manly, editor of the Wilmington *Daily Record,* the only black daily in the South, angrily replies that many lynchings for so-called sex crimes are really murders to cover up mutually consenting relations between black men and white women. His article fuels already raging fires. A. M. Waddell, the leader of the white radicals, tells thousands of whites who gather at monster political rallies that they must prevent blacks from voting by any means.

Three employees pose outside the office of the Wilmington *Daily Record,* the only black daily in the South

Go to the polls tomorrow and if you find the negro out voting, tell him to leave, and if he refuses, kill him; shoot him down in his tracks. We shall win to-morrow if we have to do it with guns.

Black women rally and encourage their men not to be intimidated by white threats:

Every Negro who refuses to register his name next Saturday that he may vote, we shall make it our business to deal with him in a way that shall not be pleas-ant. He shall be branded as a white-livered coward who would sell his liberty.

On election day, even though tens of thousands of African-Americans vote, the forces of white supremacy prove too powerful. The Democrats win throughout the state. In Wilmington, a white mob goes on a rampage after the election. Black officials are forced to resign. The mobs target Alex Manly's newspaper, destroying his printing press and burning his office. Then it turns on the black community. Reverend Allan Kirk, pastor of the Central Baptist Church, watches in horror as a massacre unfolds.

Firing began and it seemed like a mighty battle in wartime. The shrieks and screams of children, of mothers and wives caused the blood of the most inhuman person to creep. They went on firing it seemed at every living Negro, poured volleys into fleeing men like sportsmen firing at rabbits in an open field; men lay on the street dead and dying while members of their race walked by unable to do them any good.

Some members of the mob that murders at least a dozen blacks in Wilmington, North Carolina, in 1898 pose outside the burned offices of the *Daily Record*. At the top, from the left, are E. G. Parmalee, the Wilmington Chief of Police; the street where the first victim was killed; Manhattan Park where the shooting began; and Alfred Waddell, leader of the rampage.

Blacks call upon President William McKinley for federal help, but he remains silent. Thousands of African-Americans abandon the city or are forced into exile. The following year, the state legislature, now completely controlled by the Democratic Party, disfranchises blacks and imposes segregation. Many blacks blindly hold to their optimism. Bishop C. R. Harris of Charlotte confidently writes: "Thank God, North Carolina is a better state than Mississippi. The colored people are too intelligent, white people too fair, to allow or demand disfranchisement."

By 1900, North Carolina blacks are legally disfranchised, their attempt to establish a democratic, biracial political society defeated.

One reason McKinley refuses to help Wilmington's black population is that America has declared war on Spain, and he needs the South's support. The president has sent troops to occupy the then-Spanish possessions of Cuba and the Philippines. Ironically, those troops include the Buffalo Soldiers, veteran black regiments who guarded the West for more than twenty years. As they carry out America's policy of colonial occupation, imposing segregation and disfranchisement on the people of Cuba and the Philippines, McKinley tours the South preaching reconciliation between Southern and Northern whites.

As McKinley tours, every Southern state takes advantage of the Supreme Court decisions legalizing segregation and disfranchisement. Between 1890 and 1915, whites segregate blacks in courtrooms, schools, libraries, parks, theaters, hotels, residential districts, insane asylums, cemeteries, and even sidewalks. Signs reading "White" and "Colored" indicate separate facilities at restaurants, drinking fountains, boarding houses, and rest rooms. Employees are segregated in factories and in the cotton mills. Public parks are reserved for whites; circuses, fairs, and movie houses have separate ticket windows, entrances, and exits for the races. In Alabama, it is illegal for blacks to play checkers with whites. There are few restaurants and hotels for blacks. Blacks are not even allowed to live in several towns in Texas, Alabama, and Oklahoma. One resident tells a black person passing through, "We don't allow the

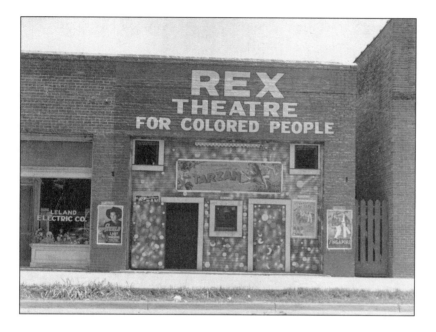

A Jim Crow movie
theater in a Southern city

sun to set on a nigger in this town—least not a live one." Mobile, Alabama, and some other communities have curfews; blacks found on the streets after 10 P.M. are arrested. Both North and South Carolina require textbooks used by white children to be kept separately from those used by blacks, and New Orleans segregates prostitutes by race in different districts. Atlanta has separate Bibles for blacks and for whites to swear on in court.

As segregation and disfranchisement spreads, the number of registered black voters drops dramatically. In 1900, 109,000 black men vote in Alabama. Ten years later, only 3,752 do. In Louisiana in 1897, there are 130,344 registered black voters. By 1904, there are 1,342. Clarendon County, South Carolina, has a population of 8,000 whites and 23,000 blacks. Of these, 6,500 whites vote, and only 237 blacks. By 1908, every Southern state legally prohibits blacks from voting. State legislatures also adopt the white primary, which means that only whites can vote in the Democratic primary. The winner of the primary is certain to win the election, as the Democrats have no political opposition in the South. Thus, even if blacks can vote, they can vote only in the meaningless general election.

Jim Crow is not only a matter of law, but also of custom. The strength of these customs vary from town to town. In some communities, segregation is so strict that a black man has to step off the sidewalk and remove his hat when a white person passes. Blacks driving a vehicle can't pass a white driver for fear they may stir up dust. Yet in other towns, blacks and white shake hands and give way to each other on sidewalks.

The mental strain on black people is often unbearable. They never know when they might inadvertently offend a white person and run the risk of being beaten, jailed, or killed. Whites expect little resistance to this oppressive system. Thus blacks have to be extremely careful of how they act in the presence of white people. If a black man speaks too loudly, whites might consider him "uppity." If he forgets to take off his hat when speaking to a white person, he is said to lack respect. And if he tries to justify his conduct, he is considered "impudent," an offense that may be punished by beatings or death.

No matter how distinguished or old a black person is, he or she is never addressed as Mr., Miss, or Mrs. by a white person. Teachers, doctors, ministers, and other distinguished black men and women are greeted as Dr. or Professor—sometimes as a term of respect, other times sarcastically.

Whites address most blacks by their first names. They also call adult black men and women "boy" and "girl." Older black people are called "uncle," "daddy," "aunty," or "mamma." Educated whites never use the word "nigger" in front of blacks or strangers. They do often use "nigruh," a combination of "nigger" and negro, or refer to blacks as "colored." Only "poor or low-class" whites call black people "niggers" to their faces.

When a black man encounters a white man he does not know, or is not on friendly terms with, he addresses him using the old slave terms "Massa" (master),

"Boss," or "Captain." If it is somebody he knows and has good relations with, he might say "Mr." and use the person's first name, as "Mr. Tom." White women are addressed as "Missus" or, if the woman is known and liked, "Miss" plus the woman's first name, as "Miss Ann." Black persons are expected to use "sir," especially when answering a question. When two black soldiers who are questioned by a white man in Mississippi, reply "Yes," instead of "Yes, sir," they are shot and killed on the spot. The white man is acquitted.

One taboo that is strictly enforced prohibits blacks and whites from eating together. One white man who claims to have excellent relationships with blacks states: "The colored people all love me where I live. Some would give their right hands to help me if I asked them. But I would starve to death before I would eat a crust of bread at a table with one of them."

The taboo of taboos is sexual relations between black men and white women. Black mothers teach their sons early to avoid white females. Many black male children are brutally murdered or castrated because a white man sees them playing too intimately, in his judgment, with a white female child. The sexual situation is so tense that black men are careful to avoid glancing at a white women seated on the porch as they walk down the street. To enforce these codes, whites use extra-legal methods such as beatings and lynchings, and legal methods such as jail and prison.

A particularly brutal form of violence against blacks is the convict lease system. Men, women, and children—some imprisoned fairly, others not—are leased to private contractors for small fees paid to the state. The contractor has absolute power of life and death over the prisoner. He can work the prisoner wherever he wants, for as long as he wants, whenever he wants, treat him in any manner he wants, and pay him nothing. Guards have the authority to beat, torture, and murder convicts at will.

States find the practice so profitable (as do corrupt judges, sheriffs, and lawmakers) that they pass laws giving blacks long sentences for minor offenses. For burglary, blacks receive sentences of 12 to 40 years, whites half as much. In 1880, a black

One of the worst features of Jim Crow is the convict lease system. Private contractors lease black prisoners from the state and work them cruelly. Some prisoners are housed in barracks on wheels as the contractors move them from place to place.

man gets 20 years for stealing a hog. A 13-year-old boy is sentenced to 20 years in Florida for stealing a horse he is too small to ride.

Ninety percent of prisoners in the South are black and young, and many are innocent of any crime. In 1880, Georgia has 1,071 black prisoners and 115 white. Many are teenagers. Out of 750 men who are sent to prison in one year in Georgia, 80 are under 14 years old, 40 are 13 years old, 27 are 12 years old, 15 are 11 years old, and 3 are 10 years old. In Texas in 1880, when the governor pardons 100 state convicts, 14 are children between the ages of 10 and 16.

Convicts are treated with unimaginable brutality. They work from four in the morning to six in the evening at hard physical labor. In Arkansas and Alabama, convicts are forced to work through the winter without shoes. In both states, a three-man team is required to mine a certain amount of coal a day or else the group is severely whipped. In Tennessee, convicts work almost naked in swamp water up to their knees. Their ankles are bound together by chains that tear into their flesh.

The death rate is extremely high. Few men survive more than 10 years in a prison camp. While it is rare for white men sentenced to convict lease groups to receive more than a 10-year sentence, many black prisoners receive from 15 to 25 years for the same crimes. In Mississippi, between 1880 and 1885, the death rate for black prisoners is between 11 and 17 percent. For white convicts it is half that. In Arkansas, the death rate in 1887 is 25 percent. And in 1870 in Alabama, 40 percent. In a Texas wood-cutting camp fewer than half the prisoners survive two years. Not all those who die are worked to death. An investigation in Arkansas uncovers the bodies of 70 prisoners tortured to death.

Convicts who fail to keep up with the rhythm of work are beaten. Some receive 10 licks on their bare backs with a leather strap. The beatings draw blood, and salt is rubbed into the wounds to intensify the pain. Black prisoners receive as many as 47 lashes, while whites receive no more than 25. The most brutal punishment is the sweat box, a small metal container that stands in the sun. The box is too small for a person to either sit or stand up in. Crouching is the only possible position. The convict is locked in the box for days in the boiling sun, with only a glass of water and some corn bread every 24 hours. Convicts are kept in the sweat box for days and many die.

Inspections of convict lease camps are rare, but when they do occur, the reports are filled with horrors. One inspector in Mississippi writes of the conditions of some inmates:

> They are filthy as a rule, as only dirt could make them, and both prison and prisoners were infested with vermin. The bedding was totally unfit for use. . . . The sick were neglected inasmuch as no hospitals had been provided. Most of them have their backs cut in great wales, scars, and blisters, some of the skin peeling off as a result of the severe beatings. They were lying there dying, some of them on bare boards, so poor and emaciated that their

bones almost came through their skin. . . . We actually saw live vermin crawling over their faces.

In Mississippi, even whites cry out for reform. The Chickasaw *Messenger* calls the convict lease system

a stain upon our manhood, a blot upon our civilization, and a stigma upon the Christianity we profess. Convicts were tortured out of all semblance of human beings; their sufferings are such that the realities of a brimstone Inferno would be a welcome relief.

Despite the outcry, the state legislatures are reluctant to end the system. Too many people profit by it, either directly or through bribes. But the protest continues to grow. In Tennessee, when mine owners bring in convict labor to keep wages low, black and white free laborers storm the prison camps at the mines, rout the guards, and free the convicts. Twice the mine owners try to use convict labor, and twice free miners release them.

Finally, the state legislature of Tennessee outlaws the convict lease system. Other states do the same. But the improvement is minimal. The convict lease system is replaced by the chain gang, and guards continue to brutalize the prisoners. The last chain gangs are not abolished until the 1960s.

EIGHT

UPLIFT

BOOKER T. WASHINGTON is a man who takes pride in turning adversity into opportunity. "An inch of progress is worth more than a yard of complaint," he says. He sees even the growing exclusion of African-Americans from American life as offering opportunities. Washington is determined to win a place for his people by encouraging them to make money. Economic success, he claims, will lead to success elsewhere. And the door to economic success remains open.

> *If today we have fewer political conventions, we have more economic gatherings. If we have fewer political clubs, we have more building and loan associations. If we have fewer men in Congress, we have more merchants and leaders in Congress.*

Despite many obstacles, tens of thousands of black men and women establish businesses and are able to have modest—and in some cases, spectacular—success

African-Americans balance the hardship of their daily lives with Sunday outings and other simple pleasures. These help them to survive the harshness of the Jim Crow world.

despite segregation. According to the National Business League, the number of businesses owned by African-Americans doubles between 1900 and 1914, from 20,000 to 40,000. The first black millionaires begin to appear. In Norfolk, Virginia, and Durham, North Carolina, and other cities, black business sections include beauty salons and barbershops, meat stores and fish markets, fruit and vegetable stands, pastry shops, clothing and shoe stores, restaurants and saloons, pharmacies and folk medicine shops, tailors and dressmakers, dry goods and jewelry stores. These enterprises bind the community together. The black communities are also centers for a black professional class that provides leadership. Black lawyers, bankers, ministers, teachers, dentists, doctors, and postal workers are often called upon for guidance and to negotiate problems with whites. Black business owners emphasize black solidarity and black pride through the National Negro Business League.

Washington promotes the efforts of men and women who have made a success in business, such as Scott Bond, a successful farmer and merchant in Arkansas; Maggie Walker, a highly regarded banker in Richmond, Virginia; and Isaiah Montgomery, the founder of Mound Bayou. In 1907, Washington visits Durham, North Carolina, to praise George Merrick, who perhaps more than any other business operator has realized Washington's ideal.

Like Washington, Merrick was a man born in slavery who worked his way to the top. In 1898, after achieving success as an owner of six barbershops, he founds an insurance company with two partners. He believes blacks should concentrate on economic success and give up politics. When the massacre occurs in Wilmington North Carolina, Merrick criticizes the black community of Wilmington: "What dif-

There are a small but growing number of prosperous African-Americans in the nineteenth century. Owning a horse and carriage, with a driver, is one of the most visible signs of success.

ference does it make to us who is elected? Had the Negroes of Wilmington owned half the city, there wouldn't anything happen compared with what did."

In 1898, Merrick forms an insurance company called the North Carolina Mutual. He hires C. C. Spaulding to run North Carolina Mutual, and the company prospers. Eventually North Carolina Mutual becomes a multimillion-dollar organization that is still in business today.

One very successful black businesses started in the nineteenth century is North Carolina Mutual Life Insurance Company.

As middle-class black men focus on economic development, middle-class black women concentrate on developing strong clubs and organizations that can reinforce positive values in their communities. Community leaders such as Mary Church Terrell and Margaret Murray Washington help organize the National Association of Colored Women (NACW), the largest national organization of women's clubs in America. Its motto is "Lifting as We Climb."

Through the local clubs, as well as through church and religious organizations, black women try to improve the quality of life of their communities. They teach school, lecture, organize literary and music clubs, and set up a variety of programs in schools to teach children better nutrition and diet. They provide social services for the elderly, children, and youth. They enter into joint ventures with white women's clubs on issues of mutual concern such as cleaner neighborhoods, healthier children, and anti-saloon campaigns. The clubs help rural black women eliminate diseases, use sewing machines, properly can foods, and make clothes for the family. They also work together in segregated local chapters of national organizations such as the Women's Christian Temperance Union and the YWCA.

In North Carolina, Charlotte Hawkins Brown wages her own campaign against Jim Crow, both as an educator and as a leader in the women's club movement of North Carolina. At a time when many black schools are stressing industrial educa-

Charlotte Hawkins Brown (right) is a leader of the black community. She founds a school for black students in Sedalia, North Carolina, at the turn of the century and fights for the voting rights of black women.

tion in order to gain white financial support (often shuttled through Booker T. Washington), Brown founds the Palmer Memorial Institute and teaches her pupils poetry, French, German, and Latin. Her purpose, in part, is to quietly subvert Jim Crow: "Recognizing the need of a cultural approach to life, absolutely believing in education through racial contacts, I have devoted my whole life to establish for Negro youth something superior to Jim Crowism."

The striving for uplift led by middle-class black men and women underscores the class structure in the African-American community. An assumption that middle-class morals and values are superior, a belief in progress, and a wish to raise up the most downtrodden of the race are motivating factors for this reform activity, especially in the NACW. Further, middle-class blacks often regard the behavior of poor blacks as a major reason for white hostility. Newspaper editor William C. Smith of Charlotte urges his middle-class readers to disassociate themselves from the "lower classes": "Our conduct should teach white people that we are not to be judged as a people by the vulgar and rough set that loafs around the streets in filth and idleness."

Like many middle-class blacks, Smith believes that if black people would live more moral lives, avoid alcohol, work hard, succeed in business, devote themselves to their families and churches, then whites would gradually accept them as equals. Smith and others fail to see that the more black people succeed, the greater the white hostility. Working-class blacks have fewer illusions about the path to advance the race. Many are willing to take a more militant stand and fight for their economic rights rather than be pushed around.

NINE

REBELLIONS, RIOTS, AND STRIKES 1900–1913

SOMETIME IN THE 1890S, Robert Charles, a semiskilled laborer, arrives in the city of New Orleans looking for work. Within a short time, he acquires a reputation as a man "not to be trifled with." He carries a gun and is willing to stand up to any man, white or black, who tries to push him too far.

When Charles arrives in New Orleans, the city is a vibrant, exciting, musical world of marching bands and string orchestras, French and Italian opera, African drumming, Haitian rhythms, Cuban melodies, and American blues, ragtime, and popular music. The city has two distinct black communities. One is the Creole black quarter, whose inhabitants trace their roots back to the time when Louisiana was a French colony, before Napoleon sold the territory to the United States. The Creole black community is Catholic and French-speaking. While some Creole blacks are wealthy, most work as skilled craftsmen—plasterers, tinsmiths, butchers, barbers, and carpenters. The other black community is English-speaking and Protestant. Some work as skilled and semiskilled labor on the docks and the river, or as unskilled, low-paying labor in the city.

Charles is surprised to discover that black dockworkers and teamsters are well organized and have struck for higher wages. Even more astonishing, white workers and black workers have organized together. When black New Orleans teamsters go on strike in 1892 for higher wages and a 10-hour day, white unions support them with a general strike. White political leaders are outraged. But white workers refuse to break the strike, and black workers win most of their demands.

Interracial coalitions around issues of mutual importance, while unusual, are not unknown in the South. To improve working conditions and receive higher wages, whites and blacks put aside racial differences and work for the common good. Sugarcane workers of both races in Louisiana and timber workers in Texas go on strike together at times, as do coal miners in Alabama and Tennessee.

Charles drifts from one low-paying nonunion job to another. In 1898, he reads about the brutal lynching in Georgia of Sam Hose, a black man who killed his landlord in a dispute over money. Hose is burned alive by a mob, his body is cut into little pieces, and part of his heart is sent to the governor. Enraged, Charles comes to the conclusion that blacks must be prepared to defend themselves: "It is the duty of every Negro to buy a rifle and keep it ready against the time they may be called upon to act in unison." Charles becomes a follower of Bishop Henry Turner, a fiery religious leader in Atlanta who is urging blacks to migrate to Liberia, an independent black republic in West Africa, founded by freed slaves from the United States. Turner has concluded there is no hope for blacks to receive justice in America.

The Negro cannot remain here in his present condition and be a man. His extermination is only a matter of time. Negroes should turn their attention to the civilization of Africa as the only hope for the Negro race.

By 1900, Charles is saving money to emigrate to Liberia and encourages others to do the same. But on a warm July night in New Orleans, as Charles and a friend,

Leonard Pierce, sit on the steps of a house waiting for their girlfriends, three white police officers try to arrest them for loitering. One officer strikes Charles, who draws his gun and shoots in self-defense. Charles is then wounded and retreats to his room. When the police come for him, a gun battle breaks out. Charles kills two policemen and flees. For several days, New Orleans is in a frenzy. Police and white mobs go on a rampage, killing and beating blacks as they search for Charles. When he is finally betrayed, a mob of 20,000 whites surrounds the house in which he is hiding and begins firing into it. Charles returns fire with expert marksmanship. Before he is shot to death, he kills five more men and wounds nineteen others.

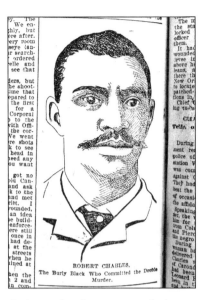

A distorted and racist image of what the white press imagines Robert Charles looks like.

After Charles's death, blacks will not speak about him. Jelly Roll Morton, the great New Orleans jazz pianist, says that a song was written about Charles but never sung.

This song was squashed very easily by the police department due to the fact that it was a trouble breeder. I once knew the Robert Charles song but I found out it was best for me to forget it and that I did in order to get along with the world on the peaceful side.

Morton, like Charles, is a man pushing against society's limits on his freedom. But unlike Charles, Morton can find relative freedom in New Orleans as a musician—one of the great musical geniuses to emerge in New Orleans at the turn of the century. A virtuoso piano player, he is one of the inventors of a new musical form—jazz.

The headlines of a New Orleans newspaper announce the death of Robert Charles in a shoot-out.

Morton's real name is Ferdinand La Menthe. He grows up in the Creole black community in the 1890s. Music is a vital part of this culture, and every family teaches its children to play an instrument. But most musicians are workers who consider music a hobby; only for a few, like Jelly Roll Morton, is music a way of life. When he is fifteen, Morton is hired to play piano in a bordello in Storyville, New Orleans's red-light district. Storyville is known for its luxurious houses of prostitution, which are for white men only. Many would-be musicians hang out in Storyville to hear the music. One is a young boy who delivers coal to the houses. His name is Louis Armstrong, and one day he will become the greatest trumpet player of his time. Another is the gifted clarinetist Sidney Bechet.

The music, it was the onliest thing that counted. The music was having a time for itself. It was moving. It was being free and natural. All the beauty that's ever been. The blues and the spirituals and the waiting and the suffering. That's all inside the music. And when the music is played right, it does an explaining of all those things. Me, I wanted to explain myself so bad. I wanted to have myself understood. And the music, it can do that. The music, its my whole story.

Jazz is only one of the musical forms African-Americans are creating. In the delta regions of Mississippi, the blues is created by rural blacks. It comes out of church music and work songs and is sung by people everywhere—in the fields, at

New Orleans is a center of African-American music. By 1900, the city is famous for its jazz bands.

work, at home, in juke joints, on chain gangs and prisons, walking along a road, riding a mule or train. Sidney Bechet first hears it as a teenager being held overnight in a Texas jail for walking in a white neighborhood. A prisoner sings the blues to express the injustice of the world.

The way he sang it was more than just a man. He was like every man that's been done wrong. Inside of him he's got the memory of all the wrong that's been done to my people.

> *"Got me accused of murder. I never harmed a man.*
> *Got me accused of forgery, can't even write my name.*
> *Bad luck, bad luck is killin' me.*
> *I just can't stand no more of this third degree."*

People sing the blues about every possible subject: sex and lust, love found and lost, going away and coming home, driving mules and riding horses, working on the farm and in the levee. Rambling through the Deep South, blues singers find in the music a sense of freedom rarely experienced in the South. Eventually many blues and jazz musicians will leave the Jim Crow South and head for the cities of the North, where they will gain greater freedom.

TEN

The Emergence of W. E. B. Du Bois

ANOTHER MAN WHO IS THINKING of heading north is a professor of sociology at the University of Atlanta, W. E. B. Du Bois. By 1900, Du Bois is considered the foremost African-American scholar in America. But despite his reputation, he is thinking of giving up academic life. Like Robert Charles, Du Bois is enraged by the brutal lynching of Sam Hose.

> At a time when my studies were most successful, there cut across my plan as a social scientist, a red ray which could not be ignored. Sam Hose had been lynched and his knuckles were on exhibition at a grocery store down the street. One could not be a calm, cool, and detached scientist while Negroes were being lynched.

Feeling that he can no longer live in an ivory tower in the academic world, Du Bois begins to speak out for the rights of his people. And one of the first people he

confronts is Booker T. Washington. Du Bois and a small
group of black leaders begin to challenge Washington's
philosophy and techniques.

W. E. B. Du Bois.

Washington's prestige has grown to the point
where he is considered by whites to be the spokesperson
for the black race. Washington has built a successful
power base at Tuskegee Institute in Alabama. He has
transformed Tuskegee from a poor, run-down school
for a few black children into a world-famous educational institution that will have, before his death in
1915, more than 100 buildings, 1,500 students, 200 faculty members, and an endowment of $2 million.

Washington has a genius for cultivating the support of powerful whites—the
mayor and wealthy citizens of the town of Tuskegee, the governor and legislature of
Alabama, members of Congress, and the president of the United States. He meets
and dines with Andrew Carnegie and other powerful industrialists. He assures these
leaders that blacks must subordinate themselves to whites at the present time. Even
though Washington secretly finances legal challenges to Jim Crow laws, he is regarded by many blacks as an accommodationist at best and as an "Uncle Tom" and
betrayer of his people at worst.

One major source of Washington's power comes from his ability to decide which
educational institutions will receive funds from Northern philanthropists and their
educational foundations. Many philanthropists share the Southern whites' attitudes
toward blacks. Blacks educators find themselves in a dilemma over accepting money
from foundations under these conditions. They want their students to have an education equal to that of white children, but the philanthropists will not support non-
industrial education. Only schools that provide vocational courses receive help.

There are few alternatives for blacks. Almost two-thirds of the more than 2 million black children between the ages of 5 and 14 do not attend school, because there are neither school buildings nor teachers for them. In 1890, out of 804,000 black children of high school age, only 958 are in public high schools. In the 16 former slave states, there is one black teacher for every 93 schoolchildren. In white schools, there is one teacher for every 57 students. In Mississippi in 1914, the average expenditure for white students is $14.94 and $1.86 for blacks. Black teachers are paid less than whites, usually only half as much. In one county, the pupil-teacher ratio is one teacher for 110 black students. Black students spend 137 days a year in school compared with 176 for whites.

More than 70 percent of the black students are enrolled in private institutions. While Northern philanthropists such as Julius Rosenwald of the Sears Roebuck Company donate part of the money needed to build schools, blacks contribute the rest. They give labor, land, and materials. They raise funds and take up collections, drawing from their meager incomes to pay for teachers.

Despite the obstacles, blacks continue to improve their educational skills. In 1866, perhaps one out of ten black people can read and write. By 1933, almost 60 percent are literate. In 1870, 9.2 percent of black children between the ages of five and twenty attend school. In 1930, 56 percent do. In the 1870s, the number of black students attending black colleges is in the hundreds. In the 1930s, it is well into the thousands.

Higher education is offered primarily through black liberal-arts colleges,

A mathematics class for black college students.

many of which are funded by missionary societies. Most colleges are underfunded, yet several, such as Atlanta, Fisk, Howard University, and Morehouse College, become outstanding educational institutions, due partly to their exceptional faculties.

Du Bois is one of a growing number of black educators who oppose Washington's willingness to sacrifice the academic education of black children in return for white financial support.

No secure civilization can be built in the South with the Negro as an ignorant, turbulent proletariat. By taking away their best-equipped teachers and leaders, by slamming the door of opportunity in the faces of their bolder and brighter minds, will you make them satisfied with their lot. . . . Such a waste of energy cannot be spared if the South is to catch up with civilization.

Du Bois teaches in Atlanta, an intellectual and economic center of the black South. The city boasts five black colleges, including Morehouse and Spelman. It also has one of the most prosperous black business sections in the country. Known as Sweet Auburn Street, the area is the center of activity for wealthy businesspeople such as Alonzo Herndon, who makes his fortune in insurance. The local black leaders include the militant Bishop Henry Turner, whose advocacy of black emigration to Liberia attracted Robert Charles; John Hope, future president of Atlanta Baptist (Morehouse); Eugenia Hope, his wife, a social worker who will develop a model social service program in America; and Hugh Henry Proctor, pastor of the First Congregationalist Church. Under Proctor's leadership, his church organizes a number of ministries including a library, a gymnasium, a bath house, a home for young working women, and employment bureaus.

Although Du Bois has published material criticizing Booker T. Washington, it is not until 1904 that he sets up an organization to challenge the older man. Du Bois calls a meeting of prominent black leaders in the North and South who oppose

Washington's philosophy. The meeting is called the Niagara Movement because it takes place on the Canadian side of Niagara Falls. The organization is dedicated to the principle of human brotherhood and demands full social, political, and educational rights for blacks.

Two years later, at a commencement exercise at Hampton University where Washington was once a student, Du Bois attacks Washington's concept of education. Following a speech by President Theodore Roosevelt praising Hampton for its educational philosophy, Du Bois lashes out:

> *It is the animating spirit of Hampton's curriculum that is the travesty. It would make Socrates look like an idiot and Jesus Christ a crank. Hampton has become an institution where the president of the United States can, with applause, tell young men not to hitch their wagons to a star but hitch them to mules. What the race needs are not tradesmen but men and women of power, of thought, of trained and cultivated taste.*

Even as Du Bois speaks out, racial tensions are building in Atlanta. In 1906, during an intense political campaign for governor, one candidate, Hoke Smith, relies on race baiting to win. He invokes the racial massacres in Wilmington: "We can handle them [blacks] as we did in Wilmington, where the woods were black with their hanging carcasses. Shall it be ballots now or bullets later?"

Smith wins and the mood remains tense. On the evening of September 22, 1906, the Atlanta *Evening News* and the Atlanta *Journal*, in competition with each other for readership, publish editions with screaming headlines about black assaults on white women. Most of these so-called assaults later prove to be nonexistent. But the damage has been done. Some 10,000 white men and boys go on a rampage. Whenever a black person is spotted, the cry goes out for blood. Two black barbers at work make no effort to resist as the mob crashes through the doors. A brick hits one in the face, and shots are fired. Both men fall to the floor. Their clothing is torn from them as souvenirs. The mob drags black men off streetcars, stabbing and kicking them to death.

Thirteen-year-old Walter White is accompanying his father, a postman, on his delivery rounds when the riot explodes around them. They are able to pass through the mobs because of their light skin color. Others are not so fortunate. The Whites witness a crippled black man being beaten to death.

We saw a lame negro bootblack coming from Herndon's barber shop pathetically trying to outrun a mob of whites. We saw clubs and fists descending to the accompaniment of savage shouting and cursing. Its work done, the mob went after new prey. The body with the withered foot lay dead in a pool of blood in the street.

White and his father return home, prepared to defend their family and property. With guns in hand, they wait inside the dark house. When the mob appears, White sees the son of a grocer with whom his family has traded for years lead the charge, "that's where the nigger mail carrier lives! Let's burn it down!" Walter White's father turns to him.

In a voice as quiet as if he was asking me to pass the sugar, he said, "Son, don't shoot until the first man puts his foot on the lawn and then—don't you miss!" In that instant there opened up in me a great awareness. I knew then who I was. I was a negro . . . a person to be hunted, hanged, abused, discriminated against, kept in poverty and ignorance. It made no difference how intelligent, or talented, my millions of brothers and I were nor how virtuously we lived. A curse like that of Judas was on us. . . . A tension different from anything I had ever known gripped me. I was gripped by the knowledge of my identity, and I was glad of it.

As whites advance toward his house, working-class blacks in a neighboring house open fire. The mob hesitates, then retreats. According to the official reports, 25 blacks and 1 white person are killed. In reality, more than 100 are killed, many of them whites. For Du Bois, the riot reinforces his conviction to leave the university and take a stand for the rights of black people.

The Niagara Movement is soon absorbed into a new organization. In 1909 many activists come together to discuss race relations and the renewal of the struggle for black rights. Many veteran activists—Ida B. Wells, Jane Addams, and the Niagara Movement members—participate in this historic interracial gathering. In 1910, under the banner of a new organization, the National Association for the Advancement of Colored People (NAACP), these activists pledge to work for an end to segregation, and for equal rights and education, black political rights, and the enforcement of the Fourteenth and Fifteenth Amendments (requiring the states to observe the rights of all citizens, and guaranteeing the right to vote). Du Bois is the only black officer of the organization. He serves as director of publicity and research and is also the editor of the organization's magazine, *The Crisis*. The NAACP launches an anti-lynching campaign and begins working through the legal system to challenge segregation. By 1918, *The Crisis* has a circulation of 100,000 a month, and by 1921 the NAACP has more than 400 chapters. It grows to become one of the foremost civil rights organizations in the country.

ELEVEN

JIM CROW AMERICA

IN 1913, AS WOODROW WILSON takes the presidential oath of office, bands play "Dixie," and Southerners shout the rebel yell. One newspaper cheers, "The South has come back to rule the nation." Their excitement is based on the fact that Wilson is a Southerner by birth, and sympathetic to Southern racial attitudes.

Du Bois hopes their joy is hollow. During the election campaign in 1912, Wilson seeks the votes of African-Americans, promising them he will not be prejudiced against them:

> *I want to assure my fellow colored citizens of my earnest wish to see justice done to them in every manner. . . . Should I become president of the United States, they may count on me for absolute fair dealing for everything by which I could assist in advancing their interests of the race.*

With the help of black votes, Wilson and the Democrats win. After almost twenty years of Republican rule, the Democrats now control Congress and the presidency. Almost one-half of the Democrats in the Senate, two-fifths of the Democrats in the House of Representatives, and half of the members of Wilson's cabinet are Southerners. Du Bois, sensing potential trouble, urges Wilson to keep his promises:

> *We want to be treated as men. We want to vote. We want our people to be educated. We want lynching stopped. We no longer want to be herded as cattle on streetcars and railroads. In the name of that common country for which your fathers and mine have bled and toiled, be not untrue to the highest ideals of American Democracy.*

Wilson immediately makes his position clear. He refuses to reappoint to office many black diplomats and high-level employees who have held their positions for years. He allows his cabinet to impose segregation in the federal government. For the first time in the federal government's history, employees are officially segregated by race at work and in dining rooms. Blacks are not allowed to supervise white workers. Applicants for federal jobs are required to submit photographs so that race can

Coal mining is one of the few industries that hires large numbers of black workers in the Jim Crow era. Black miners are noted for their militancy and their willingness to strike for better wages and working conditions.

be determined. Blacks are not hired, except for menial jobs. When three black women employees refuse to eat in the segregated section of the dining room, their supervisor warns them that their jobs are at stake.

The segregation of the federal government outrages the black community. Wilson justifies the policy on the grounds that "It is to the advantage of the colored people themselves that they should be organized in distinct bureaus where they will center their work." The Reverend Francis Grimké verbally attacks the president for his remarks.

> *How dare the President of the United States assume to lead this nation with the great sin of race prejudice resting upon him. . . . Has he no sense of decency. What kind of man would deliberately use his great power as president to break down the self-respect of a race merely to gratify a mean, contemptible race prejudice that every right thinking man ought to despise.*

The groundswell of protest slows the administration's efforts to segregate the government. But one voice is noticeable by its silence—that of Booker T. Washington. Disillusioned by the Wilson administration, and by the rising discrimination throughout the nation, Washington justifies his silence by saying that he no longer has political influence in Washington. In 1915, he dies, and Du Bois becomes a spokesperson for the African-American community.

As America enters World War I in 1917, Du Bois supports the war effort, although he fears that black soldiers will suffer from discrimination. Blacks have a firm belief in their ability to serve in the military and more than 360,000 enlist. They agitate for the training of blacks as officers and protest the segregation and discrimination they face. Although barred from the marines and holding only menial posts in the navy, they serve in almost every branch of the army.

In August 1917, a racial explosion occurs in Houston. When a battalion of black troops is sent there, they are harassed without cause by white police. After a soldier is beaten and rumored to be dead, 100 of his companions grab their rifles and march to town, looking for the police. They began to shoot whites as they march along. When a band of white policemen and armed civilians confront them, a shoot-out takes place. When it is over, 4 black soldiers and 16 whites are dead. More than 60 men are court-martialed in three trials. At the first trial, 13 black soldiers are sentenced to death by hanging. The condemned men are denied their right to appeal to the president for commutation of their sentences. C. E. Butzer, a white soldier, is present at their execution:

> *The prisoners were sitting in two rows, back to back on folding chairs, and the hangman's knots were being adjusted. The men were droning a hymn, very soft and low. "I'm coming home, I'm coming home." It was a dolorous hymn chanted in a nasal monotone. Their last words were addressed to their white guards with whom they had become friendly. And the men of the 24th could be heard to say, "Good-bye to Company C." The condemned men were composed, looking straight ahead as the nooses and caps were slipped over their heads. They met death with neither bravado or fear but in a dignified manner.*

After the men are pronounced dead, they are placed in coffins. In each coffin, a worker places a soda-water bottle containing a typewritten slip of paper with the name, rank, and serial number, and a notation: "Died December 11, 1917. At Fort Sam Houston."

The trials continue. By the time they are over, 19 men will be hanged and 67 sent to prison, some for life. Although black soldiers routinely face hostility from white civilians, this incident has a huge impact on the black community and shakes their faith in the government.

If the war makes the situation worse for black soldiers, it works to the advantage of black civilians. With white men being drafted into the army, and European immigration restricted, Northern manufacturers need black workers. Declining wages and the persistent racism lead an estimated 400,000 African-Americans to leave the South and head north between 1916 and 1929. This migration is one of the most important social phenomena of the early twentieth century.

One of the best-paying jobs for blacks is that of Pullman car porter. Many porters send their children to college, enabling them to become community and civil-rights leaders.

Chicago is the main city of destination. The Northern black press encourages migration and the National Urban League helps the migrants. The Chicago *Defender* leads a crusade: "Every black man should leave for the sake of his wife and daughters every spot in the South where his worth is not appreciated enough to give him standing as a man and a citizen in his community." The *Defender* is sold or smuggled into every city and town in the South. Preachers read it to their congregations, barbers to their customers, the literate to the illiterate. "My people grab it like a mule grabs a mouthful of fine fodder," one man reports.

Southern whites are alarmed by the mass exodus of their labor force. Southern communities ban the *Defender*. Copies are burned. Anyone caught bringing the paper into some areas is killed; anyone caught reading it is flogged.

Once the migrants arrive safely in Chicago and find jobs, they write home urging other members of their family to join them.

I am well and thankful to be in a city with no lynching, I work in the Swift Packing Company. Work is plenty here and we are glad to work. I am so thankful the Lord has been good to me. Hurry up and come to Chicago. It is wonderful.

Among the many who leave the South for factory work are some of the region's most talented musicians and writers. Louis Armstrong, King Oliver, Jelly Roll Morton, Ethel Waters, and Bessie Smith are among hundreds who make new homes in the North. Another is the Mississippi-born Richard Wright whose childhood, spent in poverty, was sustained by a dream of one day going north and becoming a writer.

World War I is a turning point for African-Americans. As they go abroad to fight for democracy, they hold to the hope it will be extended to them in their own land. At home, a new militancy develops in the African-American community as the soldiers return with high expectations. Racial violence increases, especially as blacks and whites begin to compete for jobs and live alongside each other in Northern cities. Whites respond with race riots. In the summer of 1919, known as the "Red Summer" because so much blood flows, there are riots throughout the country. Hundreds of blacks and whites die. In the North, a terrible riot takes place in Chicago, where 35 blacks and 18 whites die. Hundreds are wounded and many hundreds more are left without shelter as property is destroyed. Acts of violence spread through the South.

In 1919, the Arkansas delta seems like the land that time forgot. Most blacks still work as sharecroppers for white plantation owners. And most plantation owners cheat their tenants out of a rightful share of the crop.

Fed up with being exploited, black sharecroppers in Phillips County organize a union they call the Progressive Farmers of America. They hire a white lawyer to sue the planters for money that is due them. On one night in October 1919, as a number of union members meet in a church to discuss their case, some whites drive up to the building and exchange shots with the blacks. One white man is killed. The confrontation triggers a race riot. For almost a week, white farmers from Arkansas and Mississippi declare open season on African-Americans. Thousands of whites hunt them down, killing perhaps as many as 200. Finally the National Guard restores order, and 122 blacks are arrested. As a mob outside the courthouse calls for blood, 12 blacks are sentenced to death; another 67 are sent to prison, some for 20 years.

One of the black farmers shot by a white mob in Phillips County, Arkansas, in 1919 lies on the ground. The death toll is officially 20, but some reports state that as many as 200 people have been killed.

The NAACP hires Colonel George Murphy, a former Civil War officer and a white attorney in Little Rock, to appeal the case. Murphy is unaware at first that Scipio Africanus Jones, an African-American lawyer also from Little Rock, is already involved in the case. Jones is an exceptional man. Born into slavery, he educated himself and earned a law degree. The NAACP arranges for Jones and Murphy to work together. Murphy dies just as the appeals begin, and Jones takes over. His main task

After the massacre, almost 700 black farmers in Phillips County are arrested by soldiers and questioned. Following a long court battle, all those imprisoned are released.

is to prevent the state of Arkansas from executing the 12 men condemned to death until the case can be appealed to the United States Supreme Court. His efforts are successful. In 1924 the Supreme Court hands down its decision in *Dempsey v. Moore* and overturns the convictions of the 12 men. The decision is based on the fact that the men were convicted in a mob atmosphere. Eventually all the convicted black farmers are freed.

Observing the blacks' struggle for their rights as American citizens, W. E. B. Du Bois sounds a call to arms. He encourages blacks to stand up for their rights, despite the sometimes violent reaction of the whites:

This country of ours, despite all that its better souls have done and dreamed, is yet a shameful land that gloats in lynching, disfranchisement, caste, brutality, and insults. But by the God of Heavens, we are cowards and jackasses, if now we do not marshal every ounce of brain and brawn to fight a sterner, longer, more unbending battle against the forces of hell in our own land. WE RETURN! WE RETURN FROM FIGHTING! WE RETURN FIGHTING! Make way for Democracy!

TWELVE

FIGHTING BACK: VICTORIES AND DEFEATS

ALL THROUGH THE 1920S, the South seems frozen in time. African-Americans continue to migrate to the North. They also make significant gains in education. Students at Fisk, Tuskegee, and Howard strike for a better academic curriculum and the end to paternalistic control. In the rural areas, local blacks, working with Northern foundations such as the Rosenwald Foundation and with county school boards, build better elementary and high schools for their children.

However the rural South is suffering from an economic depression. Then in 1929, with the stock market crash, conditions worsen throughout the entire country. African-Americans in the South face poverty and exploitation. In the Northern cities they face discrimination in employment and in unions. Many blacks, concentrated in household jobs and service occupations, lose their jobs. The South is particularly hard hit. Naomi Mitchison, an English writer, visits Arkansas and writes:

The depression makes the poor even poorer. The price for cotton falls dramatically and many farmers consider themselves lucky if they are able to keep their families fed.

I have traveled over most of Europe and part of Africa, but I have never seen such sights as I saw yesterday among the sharecroppers of Arkansas. Here are people of good stock . . . being treated worse than animals. They are dressed in rags, they barely have enough food to keep them alive, their children get no education. They are prey to diseases. I saw houses in which whole families lived in conditions of indescribable misery. . . .

Many of those forced off the land ride the rails in search of work. Clarence Norris, the nineteen-year-old son of a sharecropper, is one of them. On March 25, 1931, he is riding a freight train rattling its way through Alabama looking for work. Norris becomes involved in a fight between groups of black youths and white youths. The whites are thrown off the train. They inform the local police, who telegraph the sheriff of Paint Rock, Alabama, the next town on the train's route, to stop the freight and arrest any blacks they find. The sheriff and his posse remove nine black youths.

Although racial barriers separate white sharecroppers from black sharecroppers, both races are oppressed by landowners. The children are forced to work in the fields at an early age and thus receive little education.

They also discover two white women—Ruby Bates and Victoria Price—dressed as men. They work in the mills when there are jobs and work as prostitutes when there are none. Under pressure from the posse, the women falsely claim that the black youths raped them. Norris is taken to jail as a mob calls for his blood.

> *There was these men with guns, I don't know what they are—policemen, firemen. They had uniforms. All I remember was they had brass buttons. Some are yellin', "let's take these niggers to a tree. Let's take these niggers and hang them."*

The nine youths are tried in the town of Scottsboro, Alabama, where they are found guilty of rape. Eight are sentenced to death. A mistrial is declared in the case of the ninth, who seven members of the jury also want to execute even though he is only thirteen.

As soon as the verdict is handed down, the American Communist Party moves in.

The defendants in the Scottsboro trial, with guards and an attorney

They make the Scottsboro case famous throughout the world. They campaign in churches, in union halls, and on the streets. At the same time, Party lawyers appeal the death sentences to the United States Supreme Court, and a new trial is ordered.

As the Party fights to save the lives of the Scottsboro defendants, it also organizes workers in the cities and countryside of Alabama. In the rural areas, it forms the Sharecroppers Union. One member this Union attracts is Ned Cobb, an unusual man in the rural South. He has prospered as a tenant farmer despite the odds. Yet, he still wants his fundamental rights:

> *Ever since I've been in God's world, I've never had no rights, no voice in nothing that the white man didn't want me to have—even been cut out of book learnin'. They'd give you a good name if you is obedient to them and didn't question them. You begin to cry about your rights and the mistreatin' of you and they'd murder you.*

Organizing in the rural South is dangerous. When the sheriff tries to break up a meeting of the Sharecroppers Union at Camp Hill, Alabama, a shoot-out occurs, and several organizers are killed. The following year, another confrontation takes place in nearby Reeltown when the sheriff arrives to confiscate the property of Clifford James for failure to pay his mortgage. James is a friend of Ned Cobb's. Cobb tries to talk the sheriff out of taking James's property. When he fails, Cobb must decide whether to take a stand:

> *I thought an organization is an organization and if I don't mean anything by joinin, I ought to keep my ass out of it. I had swore to stand up for poor black farmers—and poor white farmers if they'd taken a notion to join. I've got to.*

Cobb turns to enter the house when the firing begins:

I started in the house. Took one or two steps—BOOM—Mr. Platt [the sher-iff] threw his gun on me. BOOM BOOM. Shot me two more times before I could get in the door. He filled my hind end up from the bend of my legs to my hips with shot. My feet is just sloshing with blood. I snatched out my .32 Smith and Wesson, and I commenced shooting at Platt. Good God, he jumped behind a tree, soon as that pistol fired. Every one of them officers run like the devil away from there.

Wounded, Cobb is taken to the hospital at Tuskegee. Doctors treat him but make him leave as they do not want to get into trouble with whites. Clifford James, the man Cobb had hoped to protect, is severely wounded and dies of exposure on the jailhouse floor. Cobb is captured, tried, convicted, and sent to prison for thirteen years for his role in the shoot-out. He never regrets his decision.

The black church, supported often by the labor and contributions of black women, is an important resource that enables many black people to survive the hardships of Jim Crow and the Depression.

Something done in your behalf, you've got to risk. You take such work as this.
I see more good of it than I can really explain. And I believe in stickin' to a
thing that's right until whenever my eyes is closed in death.

In 1932, Franklin D. Roosevelt is elected president of the United States on the Democratic ticket. During his first term of office, Roosevelt is slow to respond to the black community's pleas for economic assistance and a condemnation of lynching. However, in 1934 the federal government reexamines its policy of noninterference in racial matters. Eleanor Roosevelt, the president's wife, helps lead the attack against discrimination. She makes a number of public appearances with black leaders, attends civil rights conferences, speaks on the radio and writes articles attacking racial prejudice and advocating justice and fair play. Partly due to her efforts, and to a recognition of the importance of the black vote, the president begins to support blacks. Black voters favor many of Roosevelt's New Deal policies and swing away from their historical support of the Republican Party. This is a time of political regeneration in the black community, with blacks winning seats in state legislatures.

Roosevelt becomes the first president in almost sixty years to publicly condemn lynching. He is also the first to be photographed with black leaders. Under Roosevelt, for the first time in the history of America, the doors to the federal government open wide for blacks. Three times as many blacks are employed in the federal government during Roosevelt's administration as under Herbert Hoover. Blacks are given positions of political power in the government rather than token jobs. Roosevelt is said to have a Black Cabinet—a group of black advisers in key positions. Robert Vann is special assistant to the Attorney General; William Hastie and Robert Weaver serve in the Department of the Interior; Eugene Kinkle Jones of the National Urban League is adviser on Negro Affairs in the Department of Commerce; and Mary McLeod Bethune serves in the National Youth Administration and becomes a close friend to the president.

New Deal programs provide vital assistance to blacks. Black musicians, writers, and actors are admitted into the federal writers' and theater programs; black workers are hired on federal work projects; black families in the North are admitted into federal housing projects; black youths are accepted into the Civilian Conservation Corps, a semimilitary camp that pays young men to work in the forests and building roads. Federal money goes to build black schools and hospitals in the South. And destitute black people are declared eligible for federal relief. However, discrimination is common in the New Deal agencies. There are vast differences in the relief grants and salaries given to whites and blacks. Although black farmers get federal assistance, many of their grants are stolen by white landlords or lost.

By the mid-1930s, many young white Southern liberals are drawn to work in Washington by the idealism of the New Deal. Among them are Virginia and Clifford Durr, Palmer Weber, Aubrey Williams, and Clark Foreman. To some degree, they have overcome the prejudices of the South. Virginia Durr, born to a prominent Alabama family, begins to question her own racial attitudes after she attends Wellesley College in Massachusetts.

Clark Howell Foreman, son of a prominent Atlanta family, is deeply affected by a lynching he witnesses in which the "barbarism" of the South is revealed.

The Negro was . . . tied to a pine tree about 100 yards from the house. The crowd of about 3,000 people gathered around the tree in a large circle. A fire was built around the Negro's feet and lit. Neither gasoline nor kerosene was used, in order that the job might not be done too fast. The Negro yelled for mercy. The fire leaps up and seems to burn him too fast. Some hardened onlooker smolders it so that the Negro might suffer longer. Finally with a monster effort, he bends over far enough to swallow some flame. He dies amid the jeers of the crowd. The dead Negro was not spared. Fingers and toes are pulled from the scorched corpse to remind the participants of the deed. At this

*juncture a woman comes forth and asks to be allowed to shoot the Negro.
The request is granted.*

For Texas-born Jesse Daniel Ames, lynching disgraces the South. For more than a decade she has been one of a group of white Southern women who join black women and the NAACP to end mob violence in the South. In 1930, she organizes the Association of Southern Women for the Prevention of Lynching (ASWPL), a radical act for the time. The members recruit local churches, social clubs, politicians, and law enforcement officers to sign a pledge condemning lynching.

We declare lynching is an indefensible crime, destructive of all principles of government, and hostile to every ideal of religion and humanity, degrading and debasing to every person involved. We pledge ourselves to create a new public opinion in the South which will not condone for any reason whatever acts of mobs or lynchers.

When a community is threatened with a lynching, the ASWPL bombards local law-enforcement officials with telegrams, phone calls, and visits, asking them to uphold the law and protect the potential victim. Ames recalls the courage of many women who head into hostile climates where lynch mobs are gathering:

Many of the people are surly, belligerent. Women were by no means safe. They knew of the constant danger and didn't forget to pray. Many were threatened. I know women who wouldn't tell their husbands of the threat because they feared their families would make them quit work.

The ASWPL is one of a number of Southern organizations working with blacks for racial justice and equality. In 1938, Southern white liberals and a few radicals form the Southern Conference for Human Welfare (SCHW)—the most liberal Southern interracial organization of its time. In its eight years of existence, the SCHW takes a strong stand against lynching and disfranchisement, and supports justice and equal opportunities for blacks. Its membership consists of liberal politicians, black activists, government officials, college professors, radical and mainstream labor organizations, grassroots organizers, newspaper editors, and members of the clergy. Many white members ignore all Southern Jim Crow customs and shake hands with blacks, eat with them, address them respectfully—in private. But publicly most dare not challenge the system. To do so would be suicidal politically and socially and could, in some areas, lead to their murder.

One white person who does speak out against Jim Crow is Lillian Smith, a writer and a native of Georgia. She boldly criticizes both white liberals and blacks who refuse to do so.

> We must say why segregation is unendurable to the human spirit. We must somehow find the courage to say it out loud. . . . To remain silent while the demagogues, the Negro haters and the racists, loudly reaffirm their faith in segregation and the spiritual lynching which this way of life inflicts, is to be traitorous to everything that is good and creative and sane in human values. I believe that the time has come when we must take our stand.

But the white community is not yet ready to take the next step forward. Black people know that as long as the races are separated, there can never be equality. As Levi Byrd of the South Carolina chapter of the NAACP states:

> What the Negro needs is INTEGRATION, not SEGREGATION. These conditions are the exact opposites. The one affirms. The other denies. All the

blessings of life, liberty, and happiness are possible in integration, while in segregation lurk all the forces destructive of these values.

The assault on Jim Crow is building up a full head of steam.

Despite progress, Jim Crow customs and laws persist.

THIRTEEN

THE WALLS COME TUMBLING DOWN

IN THE 1930S, THE NAACP launches an attack on Jim Crow in the federal courts. But the heart of its strategy is to mobilize local people on a grassroots level to challenge the laws in their own states—and then appeal those cases to the federal courts.

The main architect of the challenge is Charles Houston, former dean of Howard University's law school and the chief counsel for the NAACP. At Howard, Houston trains a new generation of civil rights lawyers—including Thurgood Marshall, Oliver Hill, and Spottswood Robinson—who will play major roles in the legal battles against Jim Crow in the next decade. Houston believes Roosevelt's New Deal offers a real possibility for social change. For the first time since Reconstruction, the federal government is intervening in the South. Houston predicts that the justices Roosevelt appoints to the Supreme Court will be sympathetic to arguments against segregation. He leads the NAACP attack on Jim Crow laws using the Constitution as his weapon.

A new generation of African-American leaders appears. The great nineteenth-century leader, Frederick Douglass (right), is shown with Thurgood Marshall, who will continue the struggle.

By 1936, blacks in South Carolina, although still prohibited from voting in the Democratic primary, vote for president in the general election. Modjeska Simkins, one of the leaders of the NAACP, sees this as a beginning: "Voting in the general election was a way of getting people's feet wet, getting them used to the water. But we knew that nothing would come of this until we could vote in the primary, which was the only real election."

Houston challenges the white primary in the courts. At the same time, he also challenges segregation in higher education. His strategy is to use the historic *Plessy v. Ferguson* case of 1898—in which segregation was upheld—as a weapon *against* segregation. In *Plessy v. Ferguson,* the Supreme Court ruled that a state can segregate as long as it provides equal facilities for both races. It is obvious that black facilities are unequal and Houston asks the court to rule that blacks have to be admitted to white institutions if facilities are unequal. When Lloyd Gaines, a college graduate, applies to the University of Missouri's all-white law school in the 1930s, he is refused on the grounds of race. The denial is challenged in the courts. In 1938, the Supreme Court rules that unless there is a black law school of equal quality in Missouri, Gaines has to be admitted.

The NAACP strategy succeeds. Over the next five years, the court orders a number of states either to admit blacks to its graduate schools or to build schools equal in quality to those of whites. Since many states cannot afford to build graduate schools for blacks, they quietly allow blacks to enter.

But while the NAACP legal victories chip away at the edges of Jim Crow, the main fortress still seems impregnable. When America enters World War II, blacks demand their full rights as American citizens. They are quick to point out the hypocrisy of Americans fighting a war against intolerance and for freedom abroad while defending segregation at home. The armed forces are segregated. The marines refuse to admit blacks, and the other service branches use them only in menial jobs. On the home front, blacks are refused jobs in defense plants. Racial

World War II has a profound impact on black soldiers. As they fight against fascism abroad, they become all the more eager to fight for their rights at home.

tensions increase in the South. Demagogues stir the flames of racial prejudice. Beatings, near-riots, and lynchings occur as whites desperately fight to drive back challenges to segregation.

A. Philip Randolph, a powerful black labor leader, helps promote what the Pittsburgh *Courier* calls the Double V, or double victory, campaign: victory over fascism in Europe and Japan, and victory over Jim Crow at home.

Jim Crow is wrong and undemocratic. It is of the same cloth as Hitler's Nazism, Mussolini's fascism, and Hirohito's militarism. The old order of southern Jim Crow can, must, and will be destroyed.

In 1942, as the war rages on in Europe and the Pacific, and racial tensions rise in America, a group of leading Southern African-Americans meets in Durham, North Carolina, and makes a strong statement against segregation. The Durham Convention opposes the poll tax, the white primary, and the concept of equal accommodations; and demands an end to compulsory segregation, discrimination, and police brutality. They ask that black people be admitted to juries. They ask for the construction of black wards in public hospitals, staffed with black doctors and nurses. They do not demand an end to all segregation. In education they seek separate but equal facilities, with the emphasis on equal. But it is the most open challenge to segregation ever made by a Southern group.

Black soldiers stationed in the South often confront Jim Crow directly. They are sometimes killed for refusing to obey segregation laws—but other times, whites are forced to back down. Sergeant David Cason is part of a company of black soldiers who confront racism in rural Louisiana, when his men are refused ice cream in a rural store.

Just as the first fellows reached the door somebody inside hooked the screen. The usual shotgun-totin' cracker was suddenly standing at the back door. Not a word had been exchanged; the silence was deafening. The fellows closest to the screen headed back to the carrier. One pulled back the canvas covering the 50mm machine gun it concealed. The team that operated the gun pulled a belt of ammunition out of its box, slapped it in place, and the triggerman swung the gun around to cover the doorway of the ice cream parlor. None of us had any illusion as to what would happen when that 50mm opened up on that ice cream shack. It would cut it and everybody in half. We knew that every white regiment and division in the state would be called down upon our heads. Without a word, we had decided to make our stand. Fortunately for all concerned, the crackers inside realized these were not "niggers playing soldier." These were black men willing to kill and die. The cracker in the back door disappeared. As we filed in, the waitress, tears streaming down her face, scooped out the ice cream with trembling hands. The whole scene was like a silent movie; not one word was spoken. When the last man got his ice cream, we walked out, swung aboard our carrier; the motor started, the noise sounding like the end of the world had come. We pulled off and all the normal sounds of the countryside were once more heard.

Black workers become increasingly militant as well. As 5 million men and women enter Northern and Southern factories, many forced off their lands by automation and crop reductions, they insist upon better jobs, better pay, and union membership. During the war, almost 1 million more blacks join unions. In 1943, in Winston-Salem, North Carolina, black tobacco workers organize a union and win a strike for higher wages and better working conditions.

More jobs open up for black women. The number of women employed in local, state, and federal governments jumps from 60,000 at the beginning of the war to 200,000 by the war's end. Blacks challenge Jim Crow laws and customs as hundreds of clashes break out on buses, on streets, and in other public places.

In 1944, the impregnable fortress of Jim Crow is breached. As a result of another NAACP challenge, the United States Supreme Court, in *Smith v. Allright*, rules that the white primary is unconstitutional.

In Columbia, South Carolina, local NAACP leaders launch a major challenge to white political control. Denied membership in the regular Democratic Party, the NAACP leadership organizes a rival party—the Progressive Democrats. Osceola McKaine, a World War I veteran and militant member of the NAACP, challenges the incumbent senator, Democrat Olin D. Johnston. McKaine is the first black candidate for U.S. Senate in South Carolina since Reconstruction.

Small breakthroughs occur in many Southern cities in almost all phases of

Southern life. A white shipyard worker in Alabama is sentenced to prison for a murderous assault on a black worker. Three white police officers in Atlanta are sent to prison for murdering a black man they arrested on a false charge. Except in Mississippi and Alabama, all states remove the poll tax. Blacks vote in some cities in North Carolina, Virginia, and Tennessee. But voting is not universal, and trying to register voters is dangerous. In Haywood County, Tennessee, Elbert Williams, a thirty-five-year-old leader of a register-to-vote drive, is murdered by whites.

The Southern way of life is seriously challenged by World War II. In many industries, large numbers of black workers are hired to work alongside whites.

In July 1946, Medgar and Charles Evers lead a group of veterans to vote in the Democratic primary in their home town of Decatur, Mississippi. The Evers brothers plan to vote against Theodore Bilbo, a rabid white supremacist who is running for re-election to the Senate. When Medgar and Charles Evers and the veterans arrive at the polling place, a group of white men blocks them from registering. Many other blacks are prevented from voting that day as Bilbo campaigns on an openly racist platform, threatening force and violence:

> *The white people of Mississippi are sleeping on a volcano, and it's up to you red-blooded men to do something about it. But you and I know the best way to keep the nigger from voting. You do it the night before the election. I don't have to tell you any more than that.*

Bilbo is elected by a landslide, but African-American voters—many of them veterans—challenge his election, saying they were denied their right to vote. They force a reluctant Senate investigating committee to come to Mississippi to hold hearings on fraud. Democrats on the committee support Bilbo but are surprised to see 68 black men testify that their rights have been denied. The Republicans who control the Senate are willing to deny Bilbo his seat for political rather than moral reasons. Bilbo, who desperately wants to return to the Senate, agrees to a compromise. Because he is seriously ill and needs an operation for throat cancer, Bilbo agrees to withdraw from the Senate temporarily. He never returns. In 1947 he dies, as the world of segregation that he fought so hard to maintain begins to crumble on all sides.

In the same year that Bilbo dies, the NAACP challenges South Carolina's white primary law. The judge who hears the case in the federal district court is J. Waties Waring, a descendant of an old Charleston family. No one expects him to rule in favor of the NAACP. He admits that he once supported white supremacy. He later explains why:

White supremacy is a way of life. You grow up in it and the moss gets in your eyes. You learn to rationalize away the evil and the filth, and you see magnolias instead.

But Waring has begun to recognize the injustice of segregation. He has already ordered South Carolina to pay equal wages to black teachers and white teachers. Now he thinks it is time for South Carolina to rejoin the Union. He declares the white primary unconstitutional, saying "Racial distinctions cannot exist in the machinery that selects the offices and lawmakers of the United States; and all citizens of this state and country are entitled to cast a free and untrammeled ballot in our elections."

As the assault on segregation becomes increasingly successful, South Carolina governor Strom Thurmond announces his resistance: "I want to tell you that there's not enough troops in the army to force the Southern people to break down segregation and admit the Negro race into our theaters, into our swimming pools, and into our homes, and into our churches."

In 1948, Thurmond leads the South in a revolt against the Democratic president, Harry Truman. Truman has insisted that the Democratic Party present a strong civil rights program. Thurman and the South strongly object. A number of Southern politicians walk out of the Democratic nominating convention and form their own party. Thurmond runs as a dissident presidential candidate, but Truman easily defeats him and the Republican candidate, and is re-elected.

But Truman's victory comes at a time when the Cold War between the United States and the Soviet Union is escalating. In 1950, the Korean War begins, and anti-communism intensifies. Because the American Communist Party was in the front ranks of the battle for civil rights, many Southern politicians charge that all civil rights activists are communists. In this way they try to discredit anyone opposed to segregation in the South. But although Southern anti-communists are able to slow down the growing civil rights movement, they cannot stop it. It is an idea whose time has come.

FOURTEEN

VICTORY

AS AFRICAN-AMERICANS ASSERT their right to vote in increasing numbers, they also attack segregation in public education. Black children suffer greatly from inferior schools. In Clarendon County, South Carolina, the Reverend J. E. Delaine, a minister and teacher in the local schools, describes the conditions:

> *I have had children come to me wet from the rain and from the white schoolbus splashing mud and water on them when I did not have a stick of wood or other fuel to make a fire and warm their bodies. I have seen children from the white schoolbus spit out the window on the little helpless Negro children coming to my school.*

While there are thirty buses for white children in Clarendon County, there are none for black. Some high school students must walk nine miles each way to attend classes. When Delaine asks the county for a schoolbus, he is refused.

Delaine meets with the chief attorney for the NAACP, Thurgood Marshall, and agrees to organize the parents to challenge segregation in South Carolina. The school board fires Delaine and his wife from their coaching positions. The board then offers to make Delaine school principal and rehire his wife if he will drop the suit. Delaine refuses. Instead, he organizes secret meetings with local parents to convince them to join the suit. Almost all depend on whites for work and credit. But after eight months, DeLaine has 107 signatures. First on the list is Harry Briggs, who has worked for almost 17 years pumping gas, repairing tires, and greasing cars at a gas station in Summerton.

My boss, he said did I know what I was doing. I said I was doing it for the benefit of my children. He didn't say nothing back. But then later, he gave me a carton of cigarettes and let me go. "Harry, I want me a boy," he said—"and I can pay him less than you."

Pressure is placed on Briggs's wife, Eliza, who works as a chambermaid at a local hotel.

They told me they are under a lot of pressure to get me to take our names off the petition. I said my name isn't on the petition, and they said, "no, but your husband's is, and you'd better tell him to take it off." I said, "He is old enough to have a mind of his own and I wouldn't do that." They gave me a week's notice.

The Ku Klux Klan starts shooting into homes. Delaine is threatened with death.

The enemies met in a certain home and planned to have Johnny Ragin kill me. Ragin confronted me with five other white men and said, "Me or you got to go to hell." My right hand in my overcoat pocket and left front finger in his face, I asked, "What did you want to go to hell for?"

Ragin backs down. But Delaine is eventually transferred by his church from Clarendon County for his own safety.

Not every white man in the county supports the tactics used to pressure blacks. One black farmer reports that a white neighbor lends him $650 to pay his mortgage: "'Go to the courthouse and get the mortgage paid,' he said. 'You can pay me back as soon as you get it. I don't want any record of this, except between me and you.'"

As the Clarendon parents file suit, there are rumblings in the quiet town of Farmville, Virginia. Farmville seems to have good race relations. Blacks and whites greet each other cordially. The town has no history of violence. A small number of blacks own land, and a number are teachers. But the color line is always present. The two races have their own churches and schools, social organizations, and ceremonies. There is anger in the black community, but few people express it.

Reverend Francis Griffin, pastor of the First Baptist Church, is determined to change conditions in the local black high school. Until 1939, Farmville refused to provide a high school for black children. When it is finally built, it has no gymnasium, no cafeteria, no auditorium with fixed seats, no locker rooms, no infirmary—while the new white high school has them all. Designed to hold 180 children, the school has 219 by the beginning of its second year. By 1947, the school is so overcrowded that classes are sometimes held in school buses and in the back of the auditorium. The parents again request a larger school. The board responds by building three tar paper shacks. A former student, Joan Johns Cobb, remembers attending classes in one of the shacks:

We used to gather around the stove to keep warm. We would wear our coats during the winter. Keep them on during class time. And it would rain and we would put buckets around the room so that when the water came through the roof, it would leak in the buckets. And sometimes it leaked on our heads.

As the classes continue to increase in size, the board continues to delay building a new school. Cobb's sister, Barbara Johns, broods about the situation.

Some of the boys in our vocational program visited the shop at the white school and came back telling us how well equipped their whole school was. The comparison made me very angry, and I remember thinking how unfair it was. I kept thinking about it all the way home, I thought about it a lot when I was in bed that night, and I was thinking about it the next day.

In 1950, Johns, then a sixteen-year-old junior, meets with four others to organize a strike. They decide to present their plan to the student body in the auditorium, without the principal or teachers present, and without consulting any adults. The students lure the principal out of the building by calling him and, pretending they are local businessowners, telling him that some students are causing trouble downtown.

Shortly before 11 A.M. on the morning of April 23, as the principal leaves school, Johns sends four students with a forged note with the principal's initials to summon all 450 students and 12 teachers to the auditorium. Among them is Barbara Johns's sister, Joan:

When we got to the assembly, Barbara came in and walked up on the stage. And I remember saying to myself, What is going on? Why is she up there? And she started to talk, and she told us about how the conditions were very bad at the school and she needed everybody's cooperation. And that in order to effect the change, we had to go on strike. And I remember sitting in my seat and cowering down because I couldn't believe it first of all, and she was talking so forcefully without any fear. And I thought, Oh my goodness, what is going to happen to us now?

The students agree to walk out. They make signs announcing the strike and march to town. For most parents, this is the first they learn of the strike. Mrs. Henry Moton is among many parents with mixed feelings.

At first, I didn't know what to think. Then after they explained to us why they did it, I did think it was right. The children had gotten so far ahead of their parents, they didn't have anything to say to us.

The white community is outraged by the strike but does not react with violence. Most believe the students are pawns in a larger conspiracy. Barbara Johns and several other students, after consulting with Reverend Griffin, write a letter to the NAACP. The letter reaches the law offices of Oliver Hill, who has been working closely with Thurgood Marshall on challenging Jim Crow laws in the federal courts. Hill is willing to take the case if the students agree to challenge segregation itself rather than just sue for better, but segregated, schools.

A few days later, as the strike continues, Oliver Hill and Spottswood Robinson arrive in Farmville to attend a meeting at the First Baptist Church. The community debates whether to support the students' desire to legally challenge the institution of segregation. Some feel that challenging segregation is going too far. Barbara Johns and Reverend Griffin argue that it is too late to turn back. "Don't let Mr. Charlie stop you from backing us," Johns pleads. "We are depending on you." The community votes to back the students. They return to school shortly after the meeting, and the NAACP files suit asking that school segregation in Virginia be struck down.

The day after the NAACP attorneys file suit, the federal district court in Charleston begins to hear arguments against segregation in the Clarendon County case. Thurgood Marshall and the NAACP ask that all schools in South Carolina be integrated.

In July 1951, the South Carolina court rules two to one in favor of the state of South Carolina. Judge Waring, who earlier declared the white primary unconstitutional, is the dissenting vote.

> *Segregation in education can never produce equality and is an evil that must be eradicated. I am of the opinion that the system of education adopted and practiced in the state of South Carolina must go. Segregation is per se inequality.*

In 1953, the Clarendon and Farmville cases are appealed to the United States Supreme Court. They are bundled together with three other cases and are collectively known as *Brown v. Topeka County Board of Education*. In 1954, the Court, echoing Judge Waring's words, declares segregation to be inherently unequal and unconstitutional.

> *We conclude unanimously that in the field of public education the doctrine of separate but equal has no place. . . . Separate educational facilities are inherently unequal.*

After seventy long years, the battle waged by African-Americans against Jim Crow has been won. In the battle, tens of thousands of African-Americans lost their lives simply because they were black. Hundreds of thousands were condemned to chain gangs and convict lease prisons simply because they were black. Millions lost opportunities to get an education and make a decent living simply because they were black. But despite the systematic attempts of white America to deny blacks their fundamental rights as citizens and human beings, enough African-Americans said "no." Their refusal to accept oppression led to their victory over segregation and disfranchisement.

The Supreme Court decision of 1954 was only the beginning. There were fiercer battles yet to be fought during the Civil Rights Era as African-Americans strove to obtain those rights now guaranteed by the court. The victory over legalized Jim Crow proved to be a major triumph, not only for African-Americans, but for all Americans.

In 1954, as a result of lawsuits by the parents of high school students in five states, the Supreme Court rules segregation in education is unconstitutional. From this moment, commemorated by a gathering of Farmville students, families, and supporters, legalized Jim Crow is dead.

EPILOGUE

THE SUPREME COURT DECISION declaring segregation in schools illegal is the beginning of a new battle. African-Americans will struggle for another twenty years to exercise the legal rights they win in 1954. Throughout much of the South, whites resist every black attempt to remove racial barriers. In some communities, they close schools rather than integrate. In other communities, they send their children to all-white private schools rather than public schools. When blacks demonstrate for their rights, they are greeted with police, fire hoses, and attack dogs. Tens of thousands go to jail. White students and black students from the North join black protestors in the South. The Ku Klux Klan and other white radical groups murder demonstrators. But the struggle continues.

There are law-abiding citizens in the South as well. In hundreds of communities, schools are integrated in a quiet and orderly way. Many Southern whites don't like it, but they respect the law. Even as some counties resist registering black voters, others open their books willingly. Governors who tried to stop black students from entering schools now begin to visit black communities to shake hands and ask people for their votes. By the 1970s, most racial barriers have fallen throughout the South. Blacks sit where they want in buses, are served in restaurants, attend schools, register in hotels, and shop in the stores of their choice. They receive better treatment in courts and in jails.

With the spotlight on the South, the North often escapes closer scrutiny. Northerners point to their advances in race relations, such as the integration of professional sports and the fact that public spaces such as buses, movie theaters, and parks, were not segregated. But beneath the surface, Jim Crow customs have always been widespread throughout the North. Before the Civil War, most Northern states pass Jim Crow laws denying blacks the right to vote, attend schools, enter hotels and restaurants, and ride on certain buses and carriages with whites. Most African-Americans are forced to live in the slums of cities and work at the most menial jobs. They are prohibited from serving on juries, testifying in court against whites, and serving as judges. Some Western states and territories even prohibit blacks from entering. As late as the 1960s, some Northern hotels and restaurants refuse to admit black people. In many cities, blacks are threatened and their homes attacked when they try to move into white neighborhoods. Many contracts used for selling and buying homes have restrictive covenants prohibiting the buyer from ever selling to blacks. Even Chief Justice William Rehnquist signs such an agreement.

If Jim Crow as a legal institution has disappeared from the American landscape, it continues to exist as part of the white American psyche. If store owners legally cannot deny blacks entrance, many continue to make it difficult or unpleasant for them to shop in their stores. Many blacks are still arrested and unjustly imprisoned, even sentenced to death because of their race. And racial murders continue to occur. In 1998, in Jasper, Texas, three white men drag a black man to death behind their truck, tearing his body apart, In Virginia, a white man beheads a black man solely because of his skin color.

Perhaps the deepest disappointment for African-Americans has been in education. Integration has proved a mixed blessing, and today many black parents feel that their children will receive a better education at an all-black school, provided it has the same resources as a white school. Whites continue to oppose affirmative-action programs designed to compensate for past inequalities in education and the workplace.

"The past isn't past," William Faulkner once wrote. "It isn't even present." Tragically, Jim Crow lingers, sometimes open and obvious, other times just below the surface of American life. In order to be rooted out, it must first be recognized. It is for that purpose that this book is written.

SOURCE NOTES

The two books listed here provide a general overview of the Jim Crow period:

Litwack, Leon. *Trouble in Mind: Black Southerners in the Age of Jim Crow*. New York: Alfred Knopf, 1998.

Woodward, C. Vann. *The Strange Career of Jim Crow*. New York: Oxford University Press, 1974.

1: THE JUBILANT DAYS OF FREEDOM

Andrews, Sidney. *The South Since the War as Shown by Fourteen Weeks of Travel and Observation in Georgia and the Carolinas*. Boston: Houghton Mifflin, 1971.

Botume, Elizabeth. *First Day Among the Contrabands*. New York: Arno Press and *The New York Times*, 1968.

Carter, Dan. *When the War Was Over: The Failure of Self-Reconstruction of the South, 1865-1867*. Baton Rouge: Louisiana State University Press, 1985.

Litwack, Leon F. *Been in the Storm So Long: The Aftermath of Slavery*. New York: Alfred Knopf, 1979.

Towne, Laura. *The Letters and Diary of Laura Towne*. New York: Negro Universities Press, 1969 (reprint).

2: CONGRESS INTERVENES

Foner, Eric, *Reconstruction: America's Unfinished Revolution*. New York: Harper and Row, 1988.

Jarrell, Hampton McNeely. *Wade Hampton and the Negro: The Road Not Taken*. Columbia: University of South Carolina Press, 1949.

Stampp, Kenneth. *The Era of Reconstruction, 1865-1877*, New York: Alfred Knopf, 1965.

Trealease, Allen. *White Terror: The Ku Klux Klan and Southern Reconstruction*. New York: 1971.

3: FROM RESTORATION TO "REDEMPTION" 1870 –1880

Logan, Rayford. *The Betrayal of the Negro: From Rutherford B. Hayes to Woodrow Wilson*. New York: Collier, 1965.

Mass Violence in America: Report from the Joint Select Committee on the Condition of Affairs of the Late Insurrectionary States 1872, House of Representatives, 42nd Congress. New York: Arno Press and *The New York Times*, 1967.

Painter, Nell Irvin. *Exodusters: Black Migration to Kansas after Reconstruction.* New York: W.W. Norton and Company, 1976.

Williamson, Joel. *After Slavery: The Negro in South Carolina During Reconstruction.* Chapel Hill: University of North Carolina Press, 1965.

Woodward, C. Vann. *Reunion and Reaction: The Compromise of 1877 and the End of Reconstruction.* New ed. New York: Oxford University Press, 1991.

4: EDUCATION: A ROAD TO FREEDOM

Anderson, James. *The Education of Blacks in the South, 1860-1935.* Chapel Hill: University of North Carolina Press, 1988.

Harlan, Lewis. *Booker T. Washington, the Making of a Black Leader.* New York: Oxford University Press, 1972.

Holtzclaw, William Henry. *The Black Man's Burden.* New York: Neale Publishers, 1915.

Washington, Booker T. *Up From Slavery (Three Negro Classics).* New York: Avon, 1965.

5: JIM CROW COMES TO TOWN

Ayers, Edward. *The Promise of the New South: Life After Reconstruction.* New York: Oxford University Press, 1992.

Barnett-Wells, Ida. *On Lynchings.* New York: Arno Press and *The New York Times*, 1969.

Cartright, Joseph. *The Triumph of Jim Crow: Tennessee Race Relations in the 1880s.* Knoxville: University of Tennessee Press, 1976.

Duster, Alfreda. *Crusade for Justice: The Autobiography of Ida B. Wells.* Chicago: University of Chicago Press, 1970.

Rabinowitz, Howard. *Race Relations in the Urban South, 1865-1890.* New York: Oxford University Press, 1978.

Woodward, C, Vann. *Origins of the New South 1877-1913.* Baton Rouge: Louisiana State University Press, 1951.

6: DISFRANCHISEMENT

Dittmer, John. *Black Georgia in the Progressive Era 1900-1920.* Urbana: University of Illinois Press, 1977.

Gaither, Gerald. *Blacks and the Populist Revolt: Ballots and Bigotry in the New South.* University: University of Alabama Press, 1975.

Hermann, Janet. *The Pursuit of a Dream.* New York: Oxford University Press, 1981.

Kousser, J. Morgan. *The Shaping of Southern Politics: Suffrage Restriction and the Establishment of the One-Party South 1880-1910.* New Haven: Yale University, 1973.

McMillen, Neil. *Dark Journey: Black Mississippians in the Age of Jim Crow.* Urbana: University of Illinois, 1989.

Raper, Arthur. *The Tragedy of Lynching.* Chapel Hill: University of North Carolina Press, 1933

Woodward, C. Vann. *Tom Watson: Agrarian Rebel.* New York: Rinehart & Co., 1938.

7: THE DARKEST TIME

Ayers, Ed. *Vengeance and Justice: Crime and Punishment in the Nineteenth Century South.* New York: Oxford University Press, 1984.

Doyle, Betram. *The Etiquette of Race Relations in the South: A Study in Social Control.* New York: Schocken, 1971.

Edmonds, Helen. *The Negro and Fusion Politics in North Carolina, 1894-1901.* Chapel Hill: University of North Carolina, 1955.

Newby, I. A. *"Jim Crow's Defense": Anti-Negro Thought in America 1900-1930.* Baton Rouge: Louisiana State University Press, 1965.

Prather, Leon H., Sr. *We Have Taken a City: Wilmington Racial Massacre and the Coup of 1898.* Rutherford, N.J.: Farleigh Dickinson University Press, 1984.

Shapiro, Herbert. *White Violence and Black Response: From Reconstruction to Montgomery.* Amherst: University of Massachusetts Press, 1988.

Steiner, Jesse, and Brown, Roy. *The North Carolina Chain Gang.* Chapel Hill: University of North Carolina Press, 1927.

8: UPLIFT

Davis, Elizabeth. *Lifting as They Climb.* Washington, D.C.: The National Association of Colored Women, 1933.

Gaines, Kevin. *Uplifting the Race: Black Leadership, Politics and Culture in the Twentieth Century.* Chapel Hill: University of North Carolina Press, 1996.

Giddings, Paul. *Where and When I Enter: The Impact of Black Women on Race and Sex in America.* New York: William Morrow, 1984.

Gilmore, Glenda. *Gender and Jim Crow: Women and the Politics of White Supremacy in North Carolina, 1896-1920.* Chapel Hill: University of North Carolina Press, 1996.

Greenwood, Janet. *Bittersweet Legacy: The Black and White Better Classes in Charlotte, 1850-1910.* Chapel Hill: University of North Carolina Press, 1994.

Higgenbotham, Evelyn Brooks. *Righteous Discontent: The Women's Movement in the Black Baptist Church 1880-1920*. Cambridge: Harvard University Press, 1993.

Jones, Jacqueline. *Labor of Love, Labor of Sorrow: Black Women, Work and Family from Slavery to the Present*. New York: Basic Books, 1985.

Lincoln, Eric. *The Black Church in the African American Experience*. Durham: Duke University Press, 1991.

9: REBELLIONS, RIOTS, AND STRIKES 1900–1913

Hair, William Ivy. *Carnival of Fury: Robert Charles and the New Orleans Race Riot of 1900*. Baton Rouge: Louisiana State University Press, 1976.

Foner, Philip. *Organized Labor and the Black Worker*. New York: International Publishers, 1974.

Lomax, Alan. *Mister Jelly Roll*. New York: Pantheon, 1965

10: THE EMERGENCE OF W. E. B. DU BOIS

Baker, Ray Stannard. *Following the Color Line: An Account of Negro Citizenship in the American Democracy*. New York: Doubleday, Page & Co., 1908.

Du Bois, W. E. B. *The Souls of Black Folk (Three Negro Classics)*. New York: Avon, 1965.

————. *The Autobiography of W. E. B. Du Bois*. New York: International Press, 1958.

Lewis, David Lwelling. *W. E. B. Du Bois: Biography of a Race*. New York: Henry Holt & Co., 1993.

Meier, August. *Negro Thought in America 1880-1915*. Ann Arbor: University of Michigan Press, 1965.

White, Walter. *A Man Called White*. New York: Arno Press, 1969.

11: JIM CROW AMERICA

Cortner, Richard. *A Mob Intent on Death: The NAACP and the Arkansas Riot Cases*. Middletown: Wesleyan University Press, 1988.

Crew, Spencer C. *Field to Factory: African American Migration 1915-1940*. Washington, D.C.: Smithsonian, 1988.

Haynes, Robert. *A Night of Violence: The Houston Riot of 1917*. Baton Rouge: Louisiana State University Press, 1976.

Tindall, George. *The Emergence of the New South: 1913-1945*. Baton Rouge: Louisiana State University Press, 1967.

12: FIGHTING BACK: VICTORIES AND DEFEATS

Ames, Jesse Daniel. *Association of Southern Women for the Prevention of Lynching, Beginning of the Movement*. Atlanta: Commission on Interracial Cooperation, 1932.

Conrad, David. *The Forgotten Farmers: The Story of the Sharecroppers in the New Deal.* Urbana: University of Illinois Press, 1965.

Carter, Dan. *Scottsboro: A Tragedy of the American South.* Baton Rouge: Louisiana State University Press, 1969.

Kelley, Robin. *Hammer and Hoe: Alabama Communists During the Great Depression.* Chapel Hill: University of North Carolina Press, 1990.

Krueger, Thomas. *And Promises to Keep: The Southern Conferences for Human Welfare, 1938-1948.* Nashville: Vanderbilt University Press, 1967.

Rosengarten, Theodore. *All God's Dangers: The Life of Nate Shaw.* New York: Alfred Knopf, 1975.

13: THE WALLS COME TUMBLING DOWN

Egerton, John. *Speak Now Against the Day: Degeneration Before the Ciril Rights Movement in the South.* Chapel Hill: University of North Carolina Press, 1995.

Myrdal, Gunnar. *An American Dilemma: The Negro Problem in Modern Democracy.* New York: Harper & Bros. 1944.

Sullivan, Patricia. *Days of Hope: Race and Democracy in the New Deal Era.* Chapel Hill: University of North Carolina Press, 1996.

14: VICTORY

Bartley, Numan. *The Rise of Massive Resistance: Race and Politics in the South During the 1950's.* Baton Rouge: Louisiana State University Press, 1969.

———*These Our Lives: As Told by the People and Written by Members of the Federal Writers Project of the Works Progress Administration in North Carolina, Tennessee and Georgia.* Chapel Hill: University of North Carolina Press, 1939.

Cohodas, Nadine. *Strom Thurmond and the Politics of Southern Change.* New York: Simon and Schuster, 1993.

Kluger, Richard. *Simple Justice: The History of Brown v. Board of Education and Black America's Struggle for Equality.* New York: Random House, 1977.

Lawson, Steven. *Voting Rights in the South, 1944-69.* New York: Columbia University Press, 1976.

Smith, Bob. *They Closed the Schools: Prince Edward County, Virginia, 1951-1964.* Farmville, VA: Martha E. Forrester Council of Women, 1996.

INDEX

Page numbers in *italics* refer to illustrations.

Adams, Henry, 37–38
addressing blacks and whites, 74–75
Amendment
    Fifteenth, 26–27, 96
    Fourteenth, 20, 22, 34, 96
American Communist Party, 107–8, 124
Ames, Jesse Daniel, 113
Anderson, Sidney, 14–15
Andrews, Sidney, 17
Armstrong, Louis, 88, 102
Association of Southern Women for the Prevention of Lynching (ASWPL), 113

baptismal ceremony, 56
Bechet, Sidney, 88, 89
Bilbo, Theodore, 123
"black codes," 15–16
blues, 88–89
Bond, Scott, 81
boycotts by blacks, 53, 58–60
Bourbons, the, 28
Briggs family, 126
Brown, Charlotte Hawkins, 83, 83–84

Brown v. Topeka County Board of Education, 130
Bruce, Blanche, 26
Buffalo Soldiers, 72
Bureau of Freedmen, Refugees, and Abandoned Lands. *See* Freedman's Bureau
Butzer, C. E., 100
Byrd, Levi, 114–15

carpetbaggers, *24,* 24
Carson, David, 120–21
chain gang, *53,* 78
Charles, Robert, 85–87, *87,* 88, 90, 93
churches, role of, 11, *13,* 13, 23, *31,* 43, *56,* 68, 82, 110
Civilian Conservation Corps, 112
coal miners, 98
Cobb, Joan Johns, 127, 128
Cobb, Ned, 40, 109–11
Congress intervention, 18–29
    Enforcement Acts of, 29
convict lease system, *75, 76,* 76–78
cotton, *33,* 39–40, *106*
The Crisis, 96
Cromwell, Oliver, 58–59

Davis, Cyclone, 60
Days of Jubilee, 9–17
Defender, 101
Delaine, J. E., 125–27
Democratic Party
    gaining majority of House of Representa-
        tives, 33–34
    and white supremacy, 24, 25, 27–28, 35
    in Wilmington, 68, 72
Dempsey v. Moore, 104
disfranchisement, 55–66, 72
Double V campaign, 119
Douglass, Frederick, 36–37, *39*, 57, *117*
    criticism of Isaiah Montgomery, 57
    denouncement of Republican Party, 36–
        37
Du Bois, W. E. B., 51–52, 90, *91*, 91, 93–94,
        96, 97, 98, 99, 104
    criticism of Booker T. Washington, 93–94
    on resistance, 104
    on Sam Hose, 90
    on segregation, 51–52
Durham Convention, 120
Durr, Virginia, 112

education for blacks, 12, *31*, 32, 41–47, 55–56,
        82–84, 91–93, 127, *131*, 134
    Isaiah Montgomery and, 55–56
    opportunities, 41–47
    resistance to, 47
    schools, *42*, *46*, *83*
    segregation in, 125, *131*
    Washington, Booker T. and, 43–45
1865 Convention of the Colored People of
        South Carolina, 14
Enforcement Acts, 29

Engle, J. C., 59
Evers brothers, 123

Felton, Rebecca, 69
Foreman, Clark, 112–13
Freedman's Bureau, 11, 14, 17
The Free Speech and Headlight, 52, 54
Fuller, David, 67–68

Gaines, Lloyd, 118
Gannett, William Channing, 12
Gary, Martin W., 35
Grant, Ulysses S., 25, 29, 35
Green, Ben, 56
Griffin, Francis, 127, 129
Grimké, Francis, 99

Hamburg massacre, 35
Harris, C. R., 72
Hayes, Rutherford B., 36, *37*, 37
Hill, Oliver, 116, 129
Holtzclaw family, 41–43, 45
Hope, John, 66, 93
Houston, Charles, 116, 118

jazz, 87–89, *89*
Jim Crow, 9, 48–54, 74, 133
    in Northern states, 133
    origin of term, 9, 51
Johns, Barbara, 128, 129
Johnson, Andrew, 14, 18, *19*, 21, 24–25
Jones, Scipio Africanus, 103–4

Kirk, Allan, 70–71
Ku Klux Klan, 25, *26*, 28, *28*–29, 65, 126,
        132

La Menthe, Ferdinand. *See* Morton, Jelly Roll
landownership, 14, 17, 33, 34, 39
laws
   "black codes," 15
   civil rights, 20
   federal and state discrimination, 20
Lynch, James, 26
lynchings of blacks, 52–53, 54, *61*, 61–64, *65*,
   90, 111, 112–13
   Clark Howell Foreman on, 112–13
   Ida B. Wells on, 54
   Roosevelt on, 111

Manly, Alex, 69, 70
Marshall, Thurgood, 116, *117*, 126, 129
Mays, Benjamin, 43
McKaine, Osceola, 121
McKinley, William, 72
Merrick, George, 81–82
migration to the North, 37–38, 40, 89, 101–2,
   105
   migrant jobs, *63*, 102
military
   blacks in the, *12*, 99–100, *119*, 120–21
   segregation in, 118
Mississippi Plan, 34–35
Mitchison, Naomi, 105–6
Montgomery, Isaiah, 55–58, 81
   on disenfranchisement, 57
Morgan, Albert, 31–32
Morton, Jelly Roll, 87–88, 102
Moton, Mrs. Henry, 129
Mound Bayou, 55–56, 58, 81
Murphy, George, 103

National Association for the Advancement of

Colored People (NAACP), 96, 103, 113,
   116, 118, 121, 123, 126, 129
National Association of Colored Women
   (NACW), 82, 84
National Urban League, 101, 111
New Deal, 111–12, 116
New Negro, 50, 51
Niagara Movement, 94, 96
Norris, Clarence, 106–7
North Carolina Mutual, 82, *82*

Parmalee, E. G., *71*
Party of Redemption, 27
Pinchback, P. B. S., 26, *27*
Plessy, HomÈre, 66
Plessy v. Ferguson, 66, 118
Pollard, Edward Allford, 32–33
Populism, 58, 59, 59–60, 68
Proctor, Hugh Henry, 93
Progressive Democrats, 121
Progressive Farmers of America, 103

Radical Republicans, the, 19, 20, 20–23
railroads, 49–50, *101*
   Pullman car porters, *101*
Randolph, A. Philip, 119
rape, as issue for lynchings, 61, 62, 69
Reconstruction
   Act of 1867, *21*, 21
   Congress and, 21–23
Rehnquist, William, 133
Rice, Thomas "Daddy," 51
Robinson, Spottswood, 116, 129
Roosevelt, Eleanor, 111
Roosevelt, Franklin D., 111, 116. *See also* New
   Deal

Rosenwald, Julius, 92

Sabbath schools, 43
"scalawags," 24
Scottsboro case, 107, *108*, 109
segregation, legalized. *See also* Jim Crow
    in federal government, 98–99
    in public establishments, 51, *52*, 72, *73*
    on public transportation, 48–49, 51–52, 66
    success despite, 79–84
sharecroppers, 39–40, 102–3, *107*
Sharecroppers Union, 109
Simkins, Modjeska, 118
Singleton, Benjamin "Pap," 38
slavery, freedom from, 10–11, 13
Smalls, Robert, 26, *27*
Smith, Hoke, 94
Smith, Lillian, 114
Smith, William C., 84
Smith v. Allright, 121
Southern Conference for Human Welfare
    (SCHW), 114
Spaulding, C. C., 82
Stevens, Thaddeus, *20*
Stewart, T. McCants, 30–31
Stowe, Harriet Beecher, 32
strikes, 15, 86, 121
Styles, H. H., 60
Sweet Auburn Street, 93

Terrell, Mary Church, 82
Thomas, Samuel, 17
Thurmond, Strom, 124
Truman, Harry, 124
Truth, Sojourner, 38
Turner, Henry, 86, 93

Tuskegee Institute, 43, 45, 64, 91

unions, 121
United States Supreme Court, 34, 57, 66, 104,
    118, 121, 130, 132
United States 28th Colored Troops, 9–10

Vann, Robert, 111
Vardaman, James, 57
violence against blacks, 16–17, 20–21, 25,
    34–35, 53, 59, 61–64, 70–71, 75–78,
    94–96, 99–100, 102, *103*, 103, 106–10,
    133–34, 75. *See also* Ku Klux Klan; Lynch-
    ings
    resistance to, 28–29, 70, 111
voting rights of blacks, 20, 21–22, *23*, 25–27,
    37, 56–57, 66, 73–74, 122–23, 125
    denying, 16, 18–19, 56–57, 66

Waddell, Alfred, 69, *71*
Walker, Maggie, 81
Waring, J. Waties, 123–24, 130
Washington, Booker T., 12, 43, *44*, 44–45, 58,
    64–66, 79, 81, 84, 91, 93–94, 99
    at Atlanta Cotton Exposition, 64–66
    history of, 44–45
Washington, Margaret Murray, 82
Watson, Tom, 59–60
Wells, Ida B., 48, 49, *49*, 52, 53, *54*, 54, 96
    as journalist, 52–54
    on lynchings, 54
White, Garland, 9–10
White, Walter, 95
Williams, Elbert, 122
Williams v. Mississippi, 66
Wilmington *Daily Record*, 69, *70*, 70

Wilson, Woodrow, 97–98
Winston, Robert, 68
women
 and black church, *110*
 community role of, 82–83
 as domestics, *50*

employment for, during World War II,
 121
 as teachers, 45–46, 82–83
World War I, 99, 100–102
World War II, 118–20
Wright, Richard, 102

Photographs ©: American Social History Project: 11, 13, 23, 26, 28, 31, 39, 40, 49 (CUNY);
Arkansas History Commission: 103, 104; Birmingham Public Library. Birmingham, Alabama:
98; Corbis-Bettmann: cover (Bettmann Archive); East Carolina College: 70; Harper's Weekly:
65; Hogan Jazz Archive: 89; Library of Congress: 2, 8, 12, 19, 20, 24, 27, 37, 42, 43, 53, 59, 61,
62, 69, 73, 76, 81, 92, 101, 106, 107, 110, 115, 117, 119, 122; Moorland-Springam Research
Center, Howard University: 54; Morgan County Archives, Decatur, Alabama.: 108; National
Portrait Gallery, Smithsonian Institution: 91; North Carolina Collection, University of N.C. Library at Chapel Hill: 50, 52, 63, 82; North Carolina Department of Archives: 33, 34, 71, 83;
Richard Wormser: 87, 88; Schomburg Center for Research in Black Culture: 131; The Valen-
tine Museum. Richmond, Virginia: 56, 80 (Cook Collection), 46.